# トム・ソーヤーの冒険
## The Adventures of Tom Sawyer

**マーク・トウェイン**
原著

**デイビッド・セイン**
英文リライト

**出水田隆文**
英語解説

イラスト
Tomoko Taguchi

●

日本語訳
牛原眞弓

●

ナレーション
Jack Merluzzi

本書の英語テキストは、弊社から刊行された
ラダーシリーズ『The Adventures of Tom Sawyer　トム・ソーヤーの冒険』から転載しています。

## まえがき

　『トム・ソーヤーの冒険』は、ミシシッピ川流域の小さな町を舞台にした小説です。

　ミシシッピ川はアメリカの中西部を東西に割きながら、メキシコ湾に流れる全長3780キロメートルの大河です。支流のミズーリ川を含めると、その長さは6210キロメートルになります。

　東海岸一帯に入植していた人々は、湖や運河を通って、五大湖の東の端までやってくることができました。そこから、さらに南下する人々は、ミネソタ州のイタスカ湖から発したミシシッピ川やその支流のミズーリ川などを伝って、南部へと向かったのです。逆に、交易などの目的で、南のメキシコ湾からミシシッピ川を北上する人も多くいました。ミシシッピ川は輸送路として、大変重要な川だったのです。

　その昔、新大陸で覇権を争ったイギリスとフランスが衝突し戦争となりました。その結果、フランス人の多く住むカナダ東部地域がイギリス領になると、多くのフランス系の人々がミシシッピ川を伝って南下し、ニューオーリンズなどフランス系の人々の本拠地だった地域に移住しました。

　それにより、フランス系の文化が、ニューオーリンズ一帯に住む黒人やカリブ系の人々の文化と混ざって、ジャズやブルースが萌芽します。そうした文化が、逆にミシシッピ川を北上し、カンザスシティやシカゴなどに上陸し、さらに東海岸へと伝搬していくのです。

　蒸気船が発明されると、それはミシシッピ川の重要な交通手段になりました。しかし多くの人は、bargeと呼ばれる小舟を使って、毛皮や食料を南部に向けて運んでいました。そうして川は物を運ぶ以上に、人とともに文化を運搬していったのです。

　19世紀、ミシシッピ川から西は開拓地でした。多くの開拓者が、豊かな土地を求め、幌馬車や時には手押し車で西に向かって旅立ちました。旅に必要な物

資を調達する基地として、ミシシッピ川やミズーリ川の沿岸には都市が生まれ、それが現在のセントルイスやカンザスシティへと成長したのです。

　マーク・トウェイン（1835-1910）は、こうした人々の活動によってどんどん変貌してゆく大河と、その周辺の森や平原、そして湿原を舞台にして、地方色豊かなこの『トム・ソーヤーの冒険』を執筆しました。それは、少年時代をミズーリ州の南端、ミシシッピ川に面したハンニバルで過ごした思い出の書でもあったのです。

　そこは、数千年前からネイティブ・アメリカンが居住し、独自の文化を維持していた場所でした。そして、最初はフランス系のカナダ人、そしてドイツやアイルランドなどからの移民が川を伝ってやってきました。

　南部と北部との中間に位置するこの地域は、南北戦争のときには、南軍に帰属するか、それともアメリカ合衆国の一部として残留するかをめぐり、激しい戦いがくり広がられたことでも知られています。

　彼の小説をよく読めば、そうした地域の背景があぶり出しのように見えてきます。そして、10人に1人のアメリカ人がそこから西に旅立ち、さらに多くの人がそこを経由して南北に拡散したこともあり、マーク・トウェインが小説で描く風景は、多くのアメリカ人の思い出の風景であり、ノスタルジーの泉でもあったのです。

　ですから、われわれは『トム・ソーヤーの冒険』を通してアメリカの原風景をじっくりと味わうことができるのです。

## 本書の構成

本書は、

□ 英日対訳による本文　　□ 欄外の語注
□ 覚えておきたい英語表現　□ MP3形式の英文音声

で構成されています。

本書は、マーク・トウェインの代表作『トム・ソーヤーの冒険』をやさしい英語で書きあらためた本文に、日本語訳をつけました。

各ページの下部には、英語を読み進める上で助けとなるよう単語・熟語の意味が掲載されています。また左右ページは、段落のはじまりが対応していますので、日本語を読んで英語を確認するという読み方もスムーズにできるようになっています。またシーンごとに英語解説がありますので、本文を楽しんだ後に、英語の使い方などをチェックしていただくのに最適です。

## 付属のCD-ROMについて

本書に付属のCD-ROMに収録されている音声は、パソコンや携帯音楽プレーヤーなどで再生することができるMP3ファイル形式です。一般的な音楽CDプレーヤーでは再生できませんので、ご注意ください。

■音声ファイルについて

付属のCD-ROMには、本書の英語パートの朗読音声が収録されています。本文左ページに出てくるヘッドホンマーク内の数字（01〜33）とファイル名（01.mp3〜33.mp3）がそれぞれ対応しています。

パソコンや携帯プレーヤーで、お好きな箇所を繰り返し聴いていただくことで、発音のチェックだけでなく、英語で物語を理解する力が自然に身に付きます。

■音声ファイルの利用方法について

CD-ROMをパソコンのCD/DVDドライブに入れて、iTunesやx-アプリなどの音楽再生（管理）ソフトにCD-ROM上の音声ファイルを取り込んでご利用ください。

■パソコンの音楽再生ソフトへの取り込みについて

パソコンにMP3形式の音声ファイルを再生できるアプリケーションがインストールされていることをご確認ください。

CD-ROMをパソコンのCD/DVDドライブに入れても、多くの場合音楽再生ソフトは自動的に起動しません。ご自分でアプリケーションを直接起動して、「ファイル」メニューから「ライブラリに追加」したり、再生ソフトのウインドウ上にファイルをマウスでドラッグ&ドロップするなどして取り込んでください。

音楽再生ソフトの詳しい操作方法や、携帯音楽プレーヤーへのファイルの転送方法については、ソフトやプレーヤーに付属のマニュアルで確認するか、アプリケーションの開発元にお問い合わせください。

# CONTENTS

## Scene 1

1. **A Few Words to Begin** 10
   はじめのことば

2. **Tom Gets into Trouble with Aunt Polly** 12
   トム、ポリーおばさんに叱られる

3. **Strong Wishes—Good Action** 18
   強く願えば——よい行いに

4. **Tom is Happy and Sad** 24
   トムはうれしかったり、悲しかったり

5. **Going to Sunday School** 30
   日曜学校へ行く

6. **In Church** 38
   教会の礼拝で

7. **A Talk of Devils—Happy Hours** 46
   悪魔の話と、うれしいひととき

8. **A Plan is Made** 58
   計画は万全

9. **Tom Decides What to Do** 64
   トム、心を決める

**覚えておきたい英語表現** 68

## Scene 2

9. **Indian Joe Explains** 72
   インジャン・ジョー、話をでっちあげる

10. **The Promise—The Boys are Afraid** 80
    誓い——少年たち、おびえる

11. **Tom is Worried** 84
    トム、心配する

12. **Tom is Kind** 88
    トムはやさしい子

13　The Young Pirates　96
　　小さな海賊たち

14　Island Life—Tom Quietly Leaves　102
　　島の生活――トム、こっそり抜けだす

15　Tom Learns What is Happening　108
　　トム、村のようすを知る

16　A Night Surprise　114
　　夜のハプニング

**覚えておきたい英語表現　122**

## Scene 3

17　Tom's Plan Succeeds　126
　　トムの計画が成功する

18　Tom's Wonderful Dream　132
　　トムのふしぎな夢

19　Tom Tells the Truth　142
　　トム、白状する

20　Becky Has a Problem　146
　　ベッキー、困ったことになる

21　Old Muff's Friends　152
　　マフじいさんの友だち

22　Happy Days and Bad Nights　164
　　うれしい昼と、こわい夜

23　Dead People and Ghosts　166
　　死人と幽霊

24　Sleeping Ghosts—A Box Full of Gold　174
　　眠る幽霊と金貨の箱

**覚えておきたい英語表現　184**

## Scene 4

**25** Bad Thoughts  188
不吉な考え

**26** Number Two—Huck Waits  192
「2号」で──ハックが待つ

**27** The Picnic—Indian Joe's Job  196
ピクニック──インジャン・ジョーの「仕事」

**28** The Old Man Reports—Everyone is Afraid  202
じいさんの報告─みんなの心配

**29** Lost, Then Found—But Not Saved  208
迷って見つかって──でも助からなくて

**30** Tom Tells the Story of Their Escape  212
トム、脱出のようすを語る

**31** What Happened to Indian Joe  216
インジャン・ジョーに起こったこと

**32** Mr. Jones's Surprise is Not a Surprise  224
ジョーンズじいさんのびっくり話は、びっくりじゃない

**33** Tom Makes New Plans  228
トム、新しい計画を立てる

A Few Words to End  236
終わりのことば

**覚えておきたい英語表現**  238

# Scene 1

# A Few Words to Begin

 Most of the stories in this book really happened.

One or two stories are my own and others happened to boys in my school. Huck Finn was a real boy and Tom Sawyer is made from three real boys.

My book is for boys and girls, but I hope that men and women also will read it. I hope that it will help them to remember when they were boys and girls, and how they felt and thought and talked, what they believed, and the strange things they sometimes did.

MARK TWAIN

CONNECTICUT, USA 1876

# はじめのことば

　この本に書いた話のほとんどは、実際にあったことです。
　ひとつかふたつはわたし自身の、そして他の話は、同じ学校にいた少年たちの経験です。ハック・フィンはほんとうにいた少年ですし、トム・ソーヤーは3人の実在の少年たちをもとにして生み出したものなのです。
　これは子どもたちのための本ですが、大人のみなさんにも読んでいただきたいと願っています。この本を読むことで、みなさんが少年少女だったころに思いを馳せ、どんなふうに感じ、考え、話したか、そして何を信じていたか、ときにはどんなおかしなことをやらかしたか、そういうことを思い出していただけたら幸いです。

　　　　　　　　　　　　　　　マーク・トウェイン
　　　　　　　　　　　　　　　コネチカット州　アメリカ　1876年

# 1 Tom Gets into Trouble with Aunt Polly

"Tom! When I find you, I'll—"

The old lady looked for the boy. She looked under the bed, but only the cat came out. She looked out of the door, and saw the boy running through the garden.

"You, Tom! What are you doing?"

"Nothing."

"Nothing! What's that on your face?"

"I don't know, Aunt Polly."

"Candy! I told you not to eat candy." Aunt Polly was about to hit the boy when he shouted.

"Look!"

The old lady turned and the boy ran. He quickly ran through the garden and was gone.

Aunt Polly smiled.

"That boy! I didn't want to hit him, but if he doesn't go to school, I'll make him work on Saturday. He's my dead sister's son, so I want him to be a good boy."

■look for 〜をさがす　■get into trouble 面倒を起こす　■about to まさに〜しようとしている　■make someone do （人に）〜させる

# 1. トム、ポリーおばさんに叱られる

「トム！ 見つけたら、ただじゃおかないからね——」
　おばさんが男の子をさがしていた。ベッドの下をのぞいたが、ネコが出てきただけだ。ドアの外に目をやると、男の子が庭を走っていくのが見えた。

「こら、トム！ 何してるの？」
「なんにもしてないよ」
「なんにもしてないだって！ じゃあ、顔についてるのは何なの？」
「知らないよ、ポリーおばさん」
「お菓子だね！ お菓子を食べちゃいけないって言ったじゃないの」ポリーおばさんが叩こうとしたとき、男の子が叫んだ。
「ほら、見て！」
　おばさんが後ろをふり向くと、そのすきに男の子は逃げだした。あっというまに庭を走りぬけて、いなくなってしまったのだ。
　ポリーおばさんは、くすりと笑った。
「まったくあの子ったら！ 叩きたくはなかったんだけどね。でも学校をさぼったら、土曜日に何か仕事をさせなくちゃ。亡くなった妹の子どもだから、いい子になってほしいんだよ」

## 1. Tom Gets into Trouble with Aunt Polly

Tom didn't go to school. He had a fun day and got home late. In the evening he did his homework. Sid, his brother, had already finished. Sid was a quiet boy who never got into trouble.

At dinner, his Aunt Polly asked Tom about his afternoon.

"Tom, was it warm in school?"

"Yes, Aunt Polly."

"Did you want to go swimming?"

"No, not really." Tom knew his aunt knew he hadn't been to school.

She touched his shirt. It was dry. But Tom knew what she would touch next. "We put water on our heads to cool down," he said quickly.

She believed him. She wanted to believe him.

The summer evenings were long. Tom walked along the street. He stopped when he saw a stranger, a boy a little taller than himself.

He was dressed in nice clothes and shoes.

The two boys looked at each other. When one moved, the other moved. They walked around each other, eye to eye.

"If we fight I can win!" Tom said.

"Try it."

"I can."

■never 副決して〜ない　■stranger　名見知らぬ人　■eye to eye 目と目が合う

## 1. トム、ポリーおばさんに叱られる

　トムはやっぱり学校に行かなかった。楽しく遊びほうけて、おそくに家へ帰ったのだ。宿題をするのも日が暮れてからだった。弟のシッドは、とうに終えている。シッドはおとなしい子で、面倒を起こしたりしなかった。

　夕食のとき、ポリーおばさんはトムに、その日の午後のことを尋ねた。
「トム、学校は暑かった？」
「うん、ポリーおばさん」
「泳ぎに行きたかったんじゃないの？」
「ううん、そんなに」トムはピンときた。どうやら学校に行かなかったことに気づいているらしい。
　おばさんはトムのシャツをさわった。かわいている。でも、次に何をさわるかトムにはわかっていた。そこで「頭から水をかぶったんだ、おかげで涼しくなったよ」と、あわてて言った。
　おばさんはトムを信じた。信じたかったのだ。
　夏の夕暮れは長い。トムは通りを歩いていた。すると、トムより少し背の高い、見知らぬ男の子を見かけて、立ち止まった。

　いい服を着て、いい靴をはいている。
　ふたりはお互いににらみあった。ひとりが動くと、もうひとりも動いた。目と目を合わせながら、互いに輪をかくように歩いた。
「ケンカしたら、おまえなんか、ぶったおせるんだからな！」とトムが言った。
「やってみろよ」
「できるさ」

## 1. Tom Gets into Trouble with Aunt Polly

"No, you can't."

"I can."

"You can't."

"Can!"

"Can't!"

Then Tom said, "I could win with one hand."

"Go ahead and try."

"You're afraid."

They moved closer. Then they started pushing and suddenly they were on the ground, hitting and fighting.

Tom got on top and hit the other boy hard.

"Give up."

The boy was crying.

"Had enough?!"

"Enough!" said the boy. Tom let him get up and walk away.

But when Tom turned to leave, the boy hit him with a rock. Tom ran after the boy, who ran to his home. His mother came out and told Tom to go home.

Tom got home late, and so he quietly entered through a window. But Aunt Polly was waiting for him. Sid had told her everything. Tom would have to work on Saturday.

■go ahead さあどうぞ、やってみろ　■get on top 上に乗る　■give up 降伏する

## 1. トム、ポリーおばさんに叱られる

「へん、できるもんか」
「できる」
「できない」
「できる！」
「できない！」
するとトムが言った。「片手でだって、ぶったおせるさ」
「じゃあ、ほら、やってみろよ」
「こわいんだろ」
ふたりは近づいていった。そして押し合いはじめたと思うと、いきなり地面にころがって殴ったりもみあったりした。
やがてトムがもうひとりの上に馬乗りになり、ボカボカと殴った。
「降参だよ」
男の子は泣いていた。
「まいったか？！」
「まいったよ！」と男の子。トムは男の子を離し、立ち上がって歩いていけるようにしてやった。
ところがトムが向きを変えて行こうとしたとき、男の子がトムに石を投げつけたのだ。トムは男の子を追いかけ、男の子は家まで走って逃げた。すると相手のお母さんが出てきて、帰りなさいと言ってトムを追い払った。
トムは夜おそくに家に帰り、窓からそっと部屋に入った。でもそこに、ポリーおばさんが待ちかまえていた。シッドが全部おばさんにしゃべっていたのだ。どうやらトムは、土曜日に仕事をすることになりそうだ。

# 2 Strong Wishes —Good Action

Saturday morning was a bright, sunny day.

But Tom was sad. He had to paint the fence. It was long and high. After painting for a while, Tom sat down to rest. Jim, a boy who worked for the family, came to get water.

"I'll get the water if you paint," Tom said.

"No, I was told to get water," Jim said.

"I'll give you a toy."

Jim took the toy, but suddenly Aunt Polly walked up and hit him with her shoe.

Tom started painting again and Aunt Polly went inside. But Tom began to think. Soon the other boys would laugh at him. He took everything out of his pocket. There was nothing of use. He couldn't buy help.

Then, he had an idea. He went quietly back to work.

Soon Ben came along. He was eating an apple and he walked up to Tom. Tom continued to paint and didn't look at Ben.

■walk up 歩み寄る　■come along やって来る、現れる

## 2. 強く願えば──よい行いに

　土曜日の朝は、まぶしいほどいい天気だった。
　でもトムは悲しかった。塀のペンキ塗りをしなければいけないのだ。塀は横に長くて、背も高い。しばらく塗ったあと、トムはすわりこんで休憩した。家の使用人のジムという男の子が、水くみにやってきた。
　「ペンキを塗ってくれたら、おれが水をくんできてやるよ」とトムが言った。
　「だめだよ、水をくんでくるように言われたんだから」とジム。
　「おもちゃをやるからさ」
　ジムはそのおもちゃを手に取ったが、いきなりポリーおばさんがやってきて、靴でパシリとひっぱたいた。
　トムはまたペンキを塗りだし、ポリーおばさんは家の中に入った。でも、トムはまた考えだした。もうすぐ他の連中がやってきて、おれを見て笑うだろうな。トムはポケットの中身を全部取り出した。役に立ちそうなものは何もない。これでは何かをあげて、手伝ってもらうこともできない。
　そのとき、いいことを思いついた。トムは落ち着いたようすで仕事に戻った。
　やがてベンがやってきた。リンゴをかじりながら、トムに近づいてくる。トムはペンキを塗りつづけ、ベンのほうを見なかった。

## 2. Strong Wishes—Good Action

"You're in trouble," Ben said.

Tom continued to work. Ben came closer. Tom wanted Ben's apple, but he didn't stop painting.

"You have to work, don't you?"

"Oh, Ben! I didn't see you."

"Let's go swimming. Or do you want to work?" Ben asked.

"What do you mean, work?" Tom said. "Maybe it's work and maybe it's not. But I like it."

"You like it?"

"Of course. You don't get to paint a fence every day."

Ben stopped eating his apple. Tom continued painting and then stopped to look at his work.

"Tom, let me paint a little," Ben said.

Tom thought and then said, "No, not this fence. You could help paint the back fence, but not this one."

"Let me try. Please. I'll be careful. I'll give you some of my apple."

"No, Ben."

"I'll give you all of my apple!"

■let someone do （人に）〜させる

## 2. 強く願えば——よい行いに

「おしおきだな」とベンが言った。

トムは仕事を続けた。ベンがさらに近づいてくる。トムはベンのリンゴが欲しかったが、ペンキを塗るのをやめなかった。

「仕事しなきゃいけないんだろ？」

「あれ、ベン！ 気がつかなかったよ」

「泳ぎに行こうぜ。それとも仕事がしたいのか？」とベンは聞いた。

「どういう意味さ、仕事って？」とトムは言った。「まあ、仕事かもしれないし、仕事じゃないかもしれないな。でも気に入ってるんだ」

「気に入ってるだって？」

「もちろんさ。塀のペンキ塗りなんて、毎日できることじゃないだろ」

ベンはリンゴを食べるのをやめた。トムはペンキを塗りつづけ、それからちょっと手を止めて、自分の仕事のできばえをながめた。

「トム、おれにもちょっと塗らせてくれよ」とベンが言った。

トムはしばらく考えてから、こう言った。「いや、この塀はだめだ。うらの塀を塗るんなら手伝えるかもしれないけど、この塀はだめだね」

「やらせてくれよ。頼むからさ。気をつけて塗るから。ほら、リンゴを少しあげるよ」

「だめだよ、ベン」

「リンゴまるごとあげるよ！」

## 2. Strong Wishes—Good Action

Tom gave the brush to Ben. While Ben painted in the hot sun, Tom sat under a tree eating the apple.

Other boys came along; Bill and John. They stopped to laugh, but soon they were painting too. Each one had to give Tom a toy or something to paint. In a few hours, Tom felt rich.

He didn't do anything, but the fence had been painted three times. If he had more paint, Tom would have been even richer.

Tom had learned an important thing. Work and play are the same thing. But you have to work before you can play.

■a few 少しの　■would have done ～だったであろう　■even 副 さらに、なおさら

## 2. 強く願えば――よい行いに

　トムはベンにブラシを渡した。ベンが暑い太陽の下でペンキを塗っているあいだ、トムは木陰にすわってリンゴを食べていた。
　他の少年たちがやってきた。ビルとジョンだ。ふたりは立ち止まって笑ったが、しばらくすると、やっぱりペンキを塗っていた。塗らせてもらうには、それぞれトムに、おもちゃか何かあげなければならなかった。数時間のうちに、トムは金持ちになった気がした。
　トムは何もしなかったのに、塀は3回もペンキを塗られた。もっとペンキがあったら、トムはもっと金持ちになっていただろう。

　トムは大事なことを学んだ。仕事も遊びも同じようなものだ。でも遊べるようになるまでは、仕事をしなければならないのだ。

# 3 Tom is Happy and Sad

 Aunt Polly was sitting by the window. She was sleeping and holding the cat.

"May I go and play now, Aunt Polly?" Tom asked.

"Have you finished already?"

"Yes."

"Is that true, Tom? It makes me sad when you lie."

She was surprised when she saw the fence.

"You do know how to work! Go and play now." She gave Tom a large apple, but didn't see him take a piece of cake too.

Tom ran to the village. Two groups of boys had met for a fight. Tom was the leader of one group and Joe Harper the leader of the other. But Tom and Joe didn't fight. They sat together and gave orders. When the fight was finished, they agreed to fight again on another day. Tom started to walk home alone. At Jeff Thatcher's house he saw a girl in the garden. She had blue eyes and yellow hair. Tom used to have a girlfriend called Amy Lawrence, but not any more.

■make someone sad （人を）悲しませる　■do 助本当に《動詞の強調》　■order 名指令
■used to 以前は〜した　■not any more もはや〜ない

# 3. トムはうれしかったり、悲しかったり

ポリーおばさんが窓のそばにすわっていた。ネコを抱いて眠っている。

「もう遊びにいっていい？ ポリーおばさん」とトムは聞いた。
「もう終わったの？」
「うん」
「ほんとに、トム？ もしウソだったら、あたしはがっかりだよ」
おばさんは塀を見てびっくりした。
「まあ、じょうずにできたね！ さあ、遊びにいっておいで」おばさんはトムに大きなリンゴをあげたが、トムがケーキもひとつ、こっそり取ったのには気づかなかった。
トムは村のほうへ走っていった。ふたつの軍団にわかれた少年たちが、戦争ごっこをするために集まっていた。トムが一方の軍団のリーダーで、ジョー・ハーパーがもう片方のリーダーだ。でも、トムとジョーは戦ったりしない。ふたりは一緒にすわって、指令を出すだけだ。戦いが終わると、他の日にまた戦争をすることに話が決まった。トムはひとりで家へ向かって歩きだした。するとジェフ・サッチャーの家の庭に、女の子がいるのを見かけた。青い目に黄色い髪の女の子だ。トムにはエイミー・ローレンスというガールフレンドがいたけれど、もうそんなことどうでもよくなった。

## 3. Tom is Happy and Sad

He watched until the girl looked at him, and began to jump around and walk on his hands so she would watch him more. She just walked into the house, but first she threw a flower to him.

Tom picked up the flower and put it under his shirt, near his heart.

He sat there until it got dark.

Aunt Polly thought Tom looked happy.

Later that evening, Sid, his brother, took some candy without asking. But Aunt Polly didn't believe that Sid could be bad, so she hit Tom. Later she learned she was wrong and felt sorry, but she didn't say sorry to Tom.

Tom felt very sad. He thought about dying. Then she would be sorry.

During the night he went to the river. Maybe he would kill himself in the river. Then he remembered his flower and took it out. Would the girl be sad if he died? This thought made him happy.

■walk on one's hands 逆立ちで歩く　■get dark 暗くなる　■look 動見る、～に見える　■make someone happy（人を）喜ばせる

## 3. トムはうれしかったり、悲しかったり

　トムがじっと見つめていると、女の子がこちらを向いてトムを見た。そこでトムは跳びまわったり、逆立ちで歩いたりして、なんとかもっと見てもらおうとした。女の子はすぐ家に入ってしまったが、そのまえに花をひとつ投げてよこした。
　トムはその花を拾いあげると、シャツの中の心臓の近くにしまいこんだ。

　トムはそのまま、暗くなるまでそこにすわっていた。
　ポリーおばさんも、トムはずいぶんうれしそうだと思った。
　その日の夕方おそく、弟のシッドが、おばさんにだまってお菓子を取った。でも、おばさんはシッドが悪いことをするなんて信じられなかったので、トムを叩いた。あとで自分がまちがっていたことを知って、悪かったと思ったけれど、トムにはあやまらなかった。
　トムはとても悲しかった。死んでやりたいとさえ思った。そうしたら、おばさんだって、悪かったと思うだろう。
　夜中にトムは川へ行った。なんなら川で自殺したっていいのだ。そのとき花のことを思い出して、シャツの中から取り出した。おれが死んだら、あの女の子が悲しむかな？ そう思ったら、うれしくなってきた。

## 3. Tom is Happy and Sad

On his way home he passed the Thatcher's house. There was a light on in a window. Was it her room? He sat under the window holding her flower. He would sit there and die in the cold. In the morning, she would look out the window and see him.

Suddenly the window opened. Someone threw water out the window and it fell on him.

Tom jumped up and ran away.

Sid saw his brother coming in. Tom's wild eyes made Sid too afraid to speak. But he would tell his aunt.

■die in 〜で死ぬ　■run away 逃げる　■too 〜 to do 〜すぎて…できない

## 3. トムはうれしかったり、悲しかったり

　家へ帰るとちゅう、サッチャーさんの家のまえを通った。窓に明かりがついている。あの女の子の部屋かな？　トムは花を持って、その窓の下にすわった。ここにすわったまま、こごえ死んでもかまわないや。朝になったら、女の子が窓の外を見て、おれを見つけるんだ。

　するといきなり窓があいた。その窓からだれかが水をぶちまけたので、トムの頭にバシャンとかかった。
　トムは飛びあがると、走って逃げた。
　シッドは、兄さんが部屋に入ってくるのを見ていた。トムの目つきがすごかったので、シッドはこわくて声が出なかった。でも、あとできっと、おばさんに言いつけてやろうと思った。

# 4 Going to Sunday School

It was a sunny Sunday morning. Tom was learning some words from the Bible. Sid had already finished, but Tom was slow. He was thinking about other things.

Tom was learning five verses. Some were long and some short. Tom had found five short ones. Aunt Polly's daughter, Mary, helped him learn them so he could say them without looking at the book.

Mary gave him a pen for studying as well. It was not a good pen, but it was a pen. Tom was pleased.

Then Mary helped him put on his Sunday clothes. He hoped that she would forget his shoes. But she did not.

When they were ready, the three children went to Sunday school. Mary and Sid enjoyed Sunday school, but Tom did not want to go.

At the church door Tom stopped to speak to a friend. "Billy, do you have a yellow ticket?"

"Yes."

"Will you sell it to me?"

■verse 名(聖書の)節　■as well その上、おまけに　■put on 着る、身に付ける

# 4. 日曜学校へ行く

　よく晴れた日曜の朝。トムは聖書にのっている聖句を覚えていた。シッドはとうに覚えたが、トムはなかなか覚えられない。すぐに他のことを考えてしまうのだ。
　トムは5節の聖句を覚えようとしていた。聖句には長いのもあれば、短いのもある。トムはその中から5節の短いのを見つけたのだ。ポリーおばさんの娘のメアリーが、聖句を覚えるのを手伝ってくれたので、とうとう本を見ずに言えるようになった。
　メアリーは、よく勉強したごほうびにとペンをくれた。いいペンではなかったが、ペンはペンだ。トムは喜んだ。
　それから、メアリーはトムに日曜日のための、よそ行きの服を着せた。靴をはかせるのを忘れてくれたらいいのにな、とトムは思ったが、メアリーは忘れなかった。
　用意ができたので、3人の子どもたちは教会の日曜学校へ出かけた。メアリーとシッドは日曜学校が好きだったが、トムは行きたくなかった。
　教会の入り口で、トムは立ち止まって友だちに話しかけた。「ビリー、黄色のカードを持ってるか？」
　「持ってるよ」
　「おれに売ってくれないか？」

## 4. Going to Sunday School

"What will you give me for it?"

Tom bought Billy's yellow ticket. Then Tom stopped other boys, and bought more tickets, some red and some blue. After ten minutes he went into the church.

These tickets were given for learning the Bible verses. A blue ticket was given for two. A red ticket for 20. A yellow ticket for 200. If a student learned two thousand verses, and got ten yellow tickets, the Sunday-school teacher gave the student a Bible.

It was a wonderful day when a boy or a girl received a Bible. Tom did not want the Bible. But he did want the wonderful experience of receiving it.

"Now, children," the teacher said, "sit quietly, and listen, like good boys and girls."

While the teacher was talking, three men, a lady and a girl entered the church. Tom was very happy to see the girl. He began fighting with the other boys, so the new girl would look at him and smile.

He quickly forgot the woman who threw water on him the night before.

The men and lady sat at the front of the church.

One man was Jeff Thatcher who lived in the village. Another man was his brother, the great Mr. Thatcher. He had traveled around the world and lived in the next large town.

■the night before 昨晚

## 4. 日曜学校へ行く

「かわりに何をくれるんだ？」

トムはビリーの黄色のカードを買った。それからトムは他の少年たちも引きとめて、赤やら、青やら、もっとたくさんのカードを手に入れた。そして10分後に教会の中へ入った。

このカードは、聖書の聖句を覚えたらもらえるのだ。ふたつ覚えたら青のカード。20個覚えたら赤のカード。200個で黄色のカードだ。生徒が2000個の聖句を覚えて、黄色のカードを10枚集めたら、日曜学校の先生が聖書をくれることになっていた。

男の子でも女の子でも、聖書をもらえる日は晴れがましい日だ。トムは聖書なんか欲しくない。でも、聖書をもらうという晴れがましい経験はしてみたかった。

「さあ、みなさん」と先生が言った。「静かにすわって、よく聞いてください。いい子はそうするものですよ」

先生が話していると、3人の男の人と、ひとりの女の人、そしてひとりの女の子が教会に入ってきた。その女の子を見て、トムはとてもうれしくなった。トムは他の子たちと小突きあいを始めた。そうすれば新しくやってきた女の子が、こちらを見て笑ってくれるだろうと思ったのだ。

昨夜水をぶっかけた女の人のことは、さっさと忘れることにした。

男の人たちと女の人は、教会の一番まえの席にすわった。

男の人のひとりは、村に住んでいるジェフ・サッチャーだった。もうひとりはその兄弟の、名高いサッチャーさんだ。世界じゅうを旅したことがあり、いまは大きな隣町に住んでいる。

## 4. Going to Sunday School

The teacher wanted to give a Bible to a boy or girl today, so the famous Mr. Thatcher would know that this was a fine Sunday school. But no child had enough yellow tickets.

Suddenly Tom Sawyer stood up. He had nine yellow tickets, nine red tickets, and ten blue tickets. The teacher was surprised Tom had so many tickets. He did not believe that Tom had learned two thousand verses. He did not believe that Tom had learned twelve.

The other boys watched Tom. Everyone wished they had enough tickets for a Bible.

Some boys were angry, because they had sold their tickets to Tom. He had become so rich from letting them paint the fence, he could buy their Sunday school tickets.

Now they knew they had been silly.

Tom stood next to the famous Mr. Thatcher. He put his hand on Tom's head and called him a fine little man. Tom could not speak. This was because he was a great man, but also because he was her father.

The famous Mr. Thatcher asked, "What is your name?"

"Tom."

"Is that all?"

"Thomas."

"But you have more? Another name?"

■stand up 立ち上がる　■silly 形 バカげた、おろかな

4. 日曜学校へ行く

　先生は今日、子どもに聖書をあげたいと思っていた。そうすれば有名なサッチャーさんに、ここがりっぱな教会学校だと知ってもらえるだろう。でも、黄色のカードを10枚持っている子どもはいなかった。
　するといきなり、トム・ソーヤーが立ち上がった。トムは黄色のカードを9枚、赤のカードを9枚、青のカードを10枚持っていた。トムがそんなにたくさんのカードを持っているのを見て、先生はびっくりした。トムが聖句を2000個も覚えたなんて、とても信じられない。12個覚えたと言ったって、信じられやしない。
　他の少年たちはトムを見つめた。みんな、自分も聖書がもらえるだけのカードがあればいいのに、と思っていた。
　怒っている少年たちもいた。トムに自分のカードを売ったからだ。トムはみんなに塀のペンキ塗りをさせて、たくさんのものをもらったので、今度はそれで日曜学校のカードを買うことができたのだ。
　自分たちがバカだったと、やっとわかったというわけだ。
　トムは、有名なサッチャーさんの横に立った。サッチャーさんはトムの頭の上に手をのせて、小さいのにりっぱだね、と言った。トムは何も言えなかった。それは、この人が偉大な人で、しかもあの女の子のお父さんだからだ。

　有名なサッチャーさんは尋ねた。「きみの名前はなんというの？」
「トムです」
「それだけかな？」
「トマスです」
「でも、もっとあるだろう？　他の名前はなにかな？」

## 4. Going to Sunday School

"Tell the man your other name, Thomas," said the teacher.

"Thomas Sawyer."

"You are a very good boy. Two thousand verses is a lot. And you will always be happy that you learned them. Learning makes great men and good men. You will be a great man and a good man some day, Thomas. You will remember this day and be glad that you went to Sunday school. Now, Thomas, tell me and this lady some of the Bible verses you have learned. Now, you know the names of the twelve great friends of Jesus Christ. Tell us the names of the first two."

Tom's face became red. He looked down at his feet and said nothing.

The teacher knew Tom could not answer. But Tom felt that he must speak.

"Can you tell me," said the lady.

Tom remembered two names from the Bible. He did not remember who the people were or what they had done. But the two names were always together. He shouted them now:

"DAVID AND GOLIATH!"

But David and Goliath were not friends of Jesus Christ. They were in a different Bible story, and David had killed Goliath.

Let's finish this story about Tom Sawyer in Sunday school.

■some day いつか ■now 圖今、今度こそ 圏さて、ところで

## 4. 日曜学校へ行く

「名字も言いなさい、トマス」と先生。
「トマス・ソーヤーです」
「きみはとてもいい子だね。2000個の聖句とは、じつにたくさん覚えたものだ。覚えてよかったと、ずっと思うことだろうよ。学ぶことで人は偉大になり、善良になるんだからね。きみはいつか偉大で善良な人になれるよ、トマス。そしてこの日のことを思い出し、日曜学校に通ってよかったと思うだろう。ところでトマス、わたしとこのご婦人に、きみが覚えた聖句を教えてくれないかな。そうだ、イエス・キリストの12弟子の名前は知っているね。最初に弟子になったふたりの名前を教えてくれるかい」

トムの顔は真っ赤になった。うつむいて足元を見つめ、何も言わなかった。

先生は、トムには答えられないとわかっていた。でもトムは、何か言わなければいけないような気がした。
「さあ、教えてちょうだいね」と、女の人が言った。
トムは、聖書にのっている名前をふたつ思い出した。それがどんな人で、何をしたかは思い出せない。でも、そのふたつの名前はいつも一緒にのっていた。ついにトムはその名前を叫んだ。
「ダビデとゴリアテ！」
だけど、ダビデとゴリアテはイエス・キリストの弟子ではなかった。ふたりは別の聖書物語に出てくる人だし、ダビデはゴリアテを殺したのだ。

日曜学校でのトム・ソーヤーのお話は、このへんで終わりにしておこう。

# 5 In Church

In church the people came to hear Mr. Sprague speak to them. Mr. Sprague spoke and prayed in church every Sunday.

The Sunday school children sat with their fathers and mothers. Aunt Polly sat with Tom, Sid and Mary. Aunt Polly made Tom sit far from the window and the interesting things outside.

Other people came in and sat down. There were old, young, rich and poor people. There was Mrs. Douglas, whose husband had died. She was rich and kind, and she lived in the big house on Cardiff Hill. There was Willie, the "Good Boy" of the village. He came to church with his mother. All the other mothers talked of his goodness. All the other boys did not like him.

The church became quiet.

■pray 動 祈る、お祈りをする　■far from ～から離れて

# 5. 教会の礼拝で

　教会の礼拝では、人々が、牧師のスプレイグさんの説教を聞きにやってくる。スプレイグさんは毎週日曜日、教会で説教をしたり祈ったりするのだ。
　日曜学校を終えた子どもたちが、お父さんやお母さんと一緒に席についた。ポリーおばさんは、トム、シッド、メアリーと一緒にすわっている。ポリーおばさんはトムを窓から離れたところにすわらせて、外のおもしろそうなものから遠ざけていた。
　他の人たちが入ってきて、席についた。年寄りがいれば、若い人もおり、お金持がいれば、貧しい人もいた。未亡人のダグラス夫人もいた。ダグラス夫人はお金持で、やさしくて、カーディフ丘の大きな家に住んでいた。村で「いい子」と評判のウィリーもいた。ウィリーはお母さんと一緒にやってきた。他の母親たちがみんな、ウィリーのいい子ぶりをほめそやした。そして他の子どもたちはみんな、ウィリーがきらいだった。

　教会がしんと静かになった。

## 5. In Church

They began with a song. Then Mr. Sprague prayed for many things and for many people. He prayed for the church, and little children, and other churches in the village, and then for the village, the country, and last, for people in far countries.

Tom did not enjoy hearing Mr. Sprague pray, but he knew he must be quiet.

While Mr. Sprague prayed, a flying beetle stopped on the back of the seat in front of Tom. The beetle began to clean its body. The beetle knew it was safe. Tom was afraid to touch the beetle while Mr. Sprague was praying, in case something bad happened to him. But as Mr. Sprague finished praying, Tom picked up the beetle. But his aunt saw this. She told him to let the beetle fly away.

Then Mr. Sprague began a longer talk. Tom began to count the pages as he talked. After church, Tom always knew how many pages there had been. But usually, he didn't know what had been said.

■beetle 图甲虫　■in case 万が一（〜する場合）の用心に

## 5. 教会の礼拝で

　人々はまず讃美歌を歌った。それからスプレイグさんがたくさんのことや、たくさんの人のために祈った。教会のために、小さな子どもたちのために、村の他の教会のために、それから村のために、国のために、そして最後に遠い国の人たちのために祈りをささげた。

　トムは、スプレイグさんの祈りを聞いているのはつまらなかったが、静かにしてないといけないことはわかっていた。
　スプレイグさんが祈っているとき、虫が飛んできて、トムのまえの席の背もたれにとまった。虫は自分の体をきれいにこすりだした。安全だとわかっているのだ。スプレイグさんが祈っているあいだは、バチがあたって悪いことが起こるといけないから、こわくて虫にさわれなかった。でもスプレイグさんのお祈りが終わると、トムはすぐさま虫をつかまえた。ところが、おばさんがそれを見ていた。そして虫を逃がしてやるように言った。

　それからスプレイグさんは、さらに長い説教を始めた。スプレイグさんが話しているあいだ、トムは説教の本のページを数えだした。教会の礼拝のあと、トムはいつも何ページあったか言うことができた。とはいえ、たいてい話の内容はわかっていなかった。

## 5. In Church

But this morning Tom was interested. Mr. Sprague talked about future peace in the world. Strong and weak countries would be friends. The strong countries, he said, would be like a strong, forest animal. The weak countries would be like a weak farm animal. But they would all be friends, and so kind that a little child could lead them.

Tom wanted to be that child.

Then the animal stories stopped and Tom lost interest. He remembered he had a large black beetle in a small box in his pocket. As he took the beetle out of his pocket, it hurt Tom's finger. It hurt and he dropped the beetle on the floor.

Tom put his finger in his mouth.

The beetle fell on its back, moving its legs. Tom watched it. Other people, also not interested in Mr. Sprague's talk, watched the beetle.

Then a sad dog entered the church looking for something interesting to do. He saw the large black beetle. This looked interesting and he became happy. He walked to the beetle and touched it with his nose. Suddenly the beetle hurt the dog's nose and the dog cried loudly.

■weak 形弱い　■so ~ that とても~なので…　■back 図背中

## 5. 教会の礼拝で

　でも今朝の話はなかなかおもしろいと、トムは思った。スプレイグさんは、未来にやってくる平和な世界について話していた。強い国も弱い国も仲よくなれるそうだ。強い国とは、森に住む強い動物のようなものだと、スプレイグさんは言う。そして弱い国は、牧場にいる弱い動物のようなものだ。だけどみんな友だちになって、とてもおとなしくなるから、小さな子どもでもつれて歩けるのだという。

　トムはその子どもになりたかった。

　やがて動物の話が終わると、トムはつまらなくなってきた。そのときふと、ポケットの中の小さな箱に、大きくて真っ黒なクワガタムシが入っているのを思い出した。ポケットからクワガタを取り出すと、そいつがトムの指にかみついた。痛かったので、トムは思わずクワガタを床に振り落としてしまった。

　そして、かまれた指を口にくわえた。

　クワガタはあおむけに落ちて、足をモゾモゾ動かしていた。トムはそれをじっと見つめた。他の人たちも、スプレイグさんの話がつまらないので、クワガタを見つめていた。

　そのとき、不機嫌そうな犬が、何かおもしろそうなことはないかと教会の中へ入ってきた。犬は大きくて真っ黒なクワガタを見つけた。これはおもしろそうだと、犬は喜んだ。そしてクワガタに近づき、鼻でつついた。するといきなりクワガタが犬の鼻にかみついたので、犬は大きな声でキャンキャン鳴いた。

## 5. In Church

The beetle fell on the floor, again on its back.

People who saw this laughed quietly. Tom was very happy. The dog felt silly and was angry. He played with the beetle for a while and then found a smaller beetle to play with. The tired dog forgot about the large black beetle and sat on it.

Again the beetle hurt the dog, but did not let go. Crying, the dog ran around the church. The cries became louder and louder, until the owner threw the dog out of a church window. The dog ran away.

Everyone who saw this laughed quietly.

Mr. Sprague had stopped speaking. He began again, but it was difficult. People were still laughing. Everyone was happy when it was time to go home. Tom was happy. It was good when something different happened in church. He was happy to let the dog play with his beetle. But the dog should not have run away with it.

■let go（つかんでいるものを）放す、手放す　■run away 走り去る、逃げ出す

## 5. 教会の礼拝で

　クワガタは、またあおむけに床に落ちた。
　これを見ていた人たちは、声を殺して笑った。トムはとてもうれしくなった。犬は、バカなことをしたと思って、腹を立てた。しばらくそのクワガタで遊んでいたが、もっと小さな虫を見つけて、そっちで遊びだした。やがて疲れてくると、大きくて真っ黒なクワガタのことをすっかり忘れて、その上にすわってしまった。
　もういちどクワガタは犬にかみつき、しかも今度は離そうとしなかった。犬はキャンキャン鳴きながら教会じゅうを走りまわった。鳴き声はどんどん大きくなり、とうとう飼い主が犬を窓から放り出した。犬は走って逃げていった。
　見ていた人たちはみんな、くすくす笑っている。
　スプレイグさんは話を中断していた。また話しはじめたが、どうもうまくいかない。みんながまだ笑っているのだ。家に帰る時間になると、だれもがほっとした。トムはうれしかった。教会でいつもとちがうことがあると、おもしろいものだ。犬とクワガタを遊ばせてやってよかった。でも、犬がクワガタを持っていってしまったのは、ひどいなあと思った。

# 6 A Talk of Devils
## —Happy Hours

The next morning Tom was very sad. It was the start of another week of school. He usually began this day wishing that there had been no Saturday and no Sunday.

He sat on his bed, thinking. If he were sick, he could stay home. He thought about his body, but he could not find a sick part.

Then he looked at his foot. His foot had been hurt.

He had an idea. He began to cry as if with pain.

But Sid continued to sleep.

Tom's voice grew louder. Now he thought the pain in his foot was real.

Still Sid did not wake up.

"Sid, Sid!" he shouted.

Sid sat up and looked at him. "Tom! What is wrong?"

■as if まるで〜であるかのように　■wake up 目を覚ます　■sit up 上半身を起こす
■What is wrong? どうしたの？

# 6. 悪魔の話と、
##   うれしいひととき

　次の日の朝、トムはとても悲しくなった。週の始めで、また学校が始まるからだ。月曜日になるといつも、いっそのこと土曜日も日曜日もなかったらよかったのに、と思うのだった。
　トムはベッドにすわって考えた。もし病気だったら家にいられるのにな。そこで自分の体をあちこち調べたが、具合の悪いところは見つからない。

　それから足を見た。足をケガしていたのだ。
　いいことを思いついた。トムは、いかにも痛そうに泣きだした。
　ところがシッドはグーグー眠っている。
　トムの声はますます大きくなった。そのうち、ほんとうに足が痛いような気がしてきた。
　それでも、シッドは目を覚まさない。
　「シッド、シッド！」とトムは叫んだ。
　シッドは身を起こし、トムを見た。「トム！ どうしたの？」

No answer.

Sid shouted again.

Tom said, "Oh, don't do that, Sid. It hurts me."

"I must call Aunt Polly."

"No. Don't call her." He cried loudly again. Then he said, "I will forget everything bad that you have done to me, Sid. When I am dead—"

"Oh, Tom, are you dying?"

"Give my cat with one eye to that new girl, and tell her—"

But Sid was gone. He ran to his aunt. "Oh, Aunt Polly! Tom is dying!"

"Dying? I can't believe it!"

But she ran to Tom's bed, "Tom! Tom, what is wrong?"

"It's my foot, Aunt. It hurts. The doctor must cut it off."

The old lady sat down in a chair and laughed, then cried and then did both together. Then she said, "Tom, you stop that, and get out of bed."

Tom stopped crying and the pain stopped too.

As he walked to school, he met Huckleberry Finn. Huckleberry's father was always drunk. The mothers in the village did not like Huckleberry. But all the children liked him. Everyone wanted to be like him.

■cut ~ off ~を切断する　■drunk 形酔っぱらった

## 6. 悪魔の話と、うれしいひととき

返事がない。

シッドはもういちど大声で聞いた。

トムは「おい、やめてくれ、シッド。大声を出したらよけい痛いよ」と言った。

「ポリーおばさんを呼ばなきゃ」

「だめだ。呼ばないでくれ」トムはまた大声で叫んだ。それからこう言った。「おまえがおれにした悪さは、全部忘れてやるよ、シッド。おれが死んだら——」

「えっ、トム、死にそうなの？」

「片目のネコを、あの新しくきた女の子にあげてくれ。それからこう伝えて——」

でもシッドはもういなかった。おばさんを呼びに走っていったのだ。「ねえ、ポリーおばさん！ トムが死にそうだよ！」

「死にそうだって？ そんなことあるわけないじゃないの！」

でも、おばさんはトムのベッドのところに走ってきた。「トム！ トム、どうしたの？」

「足だよ、おばさん。痛いんだ。きっとお医者さまに切り落とされるよ」

おばさんは椅子にすわって笑い、次に泣いて、最後は泣き笑いになった。そして言った。「トム、もうやめて、ベッドから出ておいで」

トムは泣くのをやめた。すると痛みも消えてしまった。

学校へ向かって歩いていると、ハックルベリー・フィンに出会った。ハックルベリーのお父さんは飲んだくれで、いつも酔っぱらっていた。村の母親たちはハックルベリーのことをきらっている。でも子どもたちはみんなハックルベリーが好きだった。だれもがハックルベリー・フィンのようになりたかった。

## 6. A Talk of Devils—Happy Hours

Tom also wished he could be like Huckleberry. He had been told never to play with Huckleberry, so he played with him as much as he could.

Huckleberry always wore old clothes that were too big for him. His hat was full of holes. His coat touched the ground. He went any place he wished. He did not sleep in a bed; he did not sleep in a house. He did not go to school or to church. He could go swimming or fishing when and where he wanted. He was the first boy to wear no shoes in the early summer. He was the last boy to wear shoes in the early winter. He never washed.

He had everything that any boy could want.

Tom said, "Hello, Huckleberry."

"Hello yourself."

"What is that?"

"Dead cat."

"Let me see, Huck. Where did you get him?"

"From a boy."

"Why do you want a dead cat, Huck?"

■as ~ as one can できるだけ~　■wore 動wear(着る)の過去　■full of ~でいっぱいである　■Hello yourself. やあ。こんにちは。《返礼のあいさつ》

## 6. 悪魔の話と、うれしいひととき

　トムも、ハックルベリーのようになれたらいいのに、と思っていた。ハックルベリーと遊んではいけないと言われていたので、できるだけいっぱいハックルベリーと遊ぶようにしていた。
　ハックルベリーはいつも、古ぼけたぶかぶかの服を着ていた。帽子は穴だらけ。上着のすそは地面につくほど長い。ハックルベリーはどこでも行きたいところへ行った。寝るのはベッドの上ではないし、家の中でさえなかった。学校にも教会にも行かなかった。好きなときに好きなところへ、泳ぎに行ったり、釣りに行ったりすることができた。夏が近づくと、どの子より真っ先に裸足になる。冬が近づくと、どの子よりおそくまで靴をはかなかった。そして、ぜったい体を洗わなかった。

　どんな少年でも欲しがるものを、ハックルベリーは全部持っていたのだ。
　トムは言った。「やあ、ハックルベリー」
　「やあ」
　「それ、なんだい？」
　「死んだネコさ」
　「見せてくれよ、ハック。どこで手に入れたんだい？」
　「男の子にもらったんだ」
　「なんで死んだネコなんか欲しいのさ、ハック？」

## 6. A Talk of Devils — Happy Hours

"To take off these warts." Huckleberry showed Tom the hard bits of skin on his hands.

"Huck, when are you going to do it?"

"Tonight. I think that they will come to get old Williams tonight."

"But they put him in the ground Saturday. The devils would take him Saturday night."

"The devils can't come until twelve. At twelve on Saturday night, it is Sunday. Devils can't come on Sunday."

"I never thought of that. Let me go with you."

"If you won't be afraid."

"Afraid! Will you come to my house and call to me? Make a sound like a cat."

"Yes. But you must answer. Another night I came to your house, and made a sound like a cat. But you never answered. And your neighbor threw rocks at me."

"Aunt Polly was watching me. But I will answer this time."

Tom quickly walked to school and sat in his seat.

The teacher looked at him. "Thomas Sawyer!"

Tom knew that trouble was coming when his full name was used.

■take off 取り外す、取り去る　■wart 名イボ　■bit 名部分、小片　■make a sound 音を立てる

## 6. 悪魔の話と、うれしいひととき

「このイボを取るためさ」ハックルベリーは自分の手の、皮膚が硬くなったところを見せた。
「ハック、いつ、イボ取りのおまじないをするんだ？」
「今夜だよ。おいら思うんだけど、きっと今夜、あいつらがウィリアムズじいさんの死体を取りに来るぜ」
「でも、土に埋めたのは土曜日だろ。悪魔が取りに来るんだったら、土曜の夜じゃないか」
「悪魔は12時までは来れないんだ。そんで土曜の夜12時といったら、もう日曜日だ。悪魔は日曜日には来れないだろ」
「それは気がつかなかったな。おれもつれてってくれよ」
「こわくなかったらな」
「こわいだって！ おれの家に呼びにきてくれよ。ネコの声を出してさ」
「いいよ。でも、ちゃんと返事しろよ。このまえも、おまえんちに行ってネコの声で呼んだのに、返事しなかったじゃないか。それでおいら、近所の人に石を投げられたんだぞ」
「ポリーおばさんに見張られてたんだよ。でも今度はちゃんと返事するからさ」
　トムはあわてて学校まで歩き、席についた。
　先生がトムをじっと見た。「トマス・ソーヤー！」
　こんなふうにフルネームで呼ばれたら、まずいことが起こると、トムにはわかっていた。

## 6. A Talk of Devils—Happy Hours

"Why are you late again?"

Tom looked around the room. He saw the new girl. No one was sitting next to her.

He said, "I STOPPED TO TALK WITH HUCKLEBERRY FINN."

Everyone was surprised.

"Thomas Sawyer, I never heard more surprising words. Take off your coat." The teacher hit him, "Go and sit with the girls!"

The new girl turned her back towards Tom. When she turned toward him, she saw an apple on the table in front of her. She moved it away. Tom moved it toward her. She moved it away again. Tom returned it. She did not move it again.

Tom began to draw a picture on a piece of paper. She tried to see it and said, "Let me see."

He showed her. It was a picture of a house. It was not good, but she thought that it was. "It is nice. Now make a man."

The man was bigger than the house.

"It is beautiful. Now make me."

He made a picture of another person.

■no one 誰も[ひとりも]（〜ない）　■turn one's back 背を向ける、そっぽを向く

6. 悪魔の話と、うれしいひととき

「どうしてまた遅刻したんだね？」
　トムは教室を見まわした。あの新しくきた女の子がいた。となりの席があいている。
　トムは言った。「とちゅうでハックルベリー・フィンに会って話してたんです」
　みんなは、それを聞いてびっくりした。
「トマス・ソーヤー、まったく、こんなあきれた話は聞いたことがないぞ。さあ上着を脱ぎなさい」先生はトムをムチで叩いた。「さあ、罰として、女子の席にすわりなさい！」
　新しくきた女の子は、トムに背を向けて無視した。しばらくしてトムのほうをちらっと見ると、目の前の机の上にリンゴがのっていた。女の子はリンゴを押しやった。トムは女の子のほうにリンゴを押しもどした。女の子がまた押しやる。トムもまた元にもどす。女の子はもう押しやるのをやめた。
　トムが紙に絵を描きだした。女の子は見ようとして言った。「ねえ、見せて」

　トムは絵を女の子に見せた。家の絵だった。うまくはなかったが、女の子は、いい絵だと思った。「じょうずね。今度は、人を描いてみて」

　トムが描いた人は、家より大きかった。
「すてきだわ。ねえ、あたしを描いてよ」
　トムはもうひとり、人の絵を描いた。

## 6. A Talk of Devils—Happy Hours

"That is very nice. I wish I could make pictures."

"I will teach you. At noon. Do you go home to eat?"

"I will stay if you stay."

"Good. What is your name?"

"Becky Thatcher. What is yours? Oh, I know. It is Thomas Sawyer."

"That is my name when I am bad. I am Tom when I am good. Please call me Tom."

Next Tom began writing something. She asked to see.

"No. You will tell what it is."

"I promise never to tell."

Tom let her pull the writing away. She read these words: "I love you."

"Oh, you bad thing!" And she hit his hand. But her face looked happy.

Suddenly he felt a hand on his ear, pulling him from the seat. He moved back to his normal seat. Everyone laughed.

Tom's ear hurt, but his heart was happy.

■pull ~ away ～をもぎ取る  ■writing 图文書  ■bad thing 悪い子

## 6. 悪魔の話と、うれしいひととき

「とってもすてき。あたしも絵が描けたらなあ」
「教えてやるよ。お昼の時間にね。家に食べに帰るの？」
「あなたがいるなら、帰らないわ」
「よし、わかった。名前を教えてくれる？」
「ベッキー・サッチャーよ。あなたは？ あ、知ってるわ。トマス・ソーヤーでしょ」
「それは悪い子のときの名前だよ。いい子のときはトムなんだ。トムって呼んでよ」

次にトムは何か字を書きはじめた。ベッキーは、見せてと言った。
「だめだよ。見たら人に言うだろ」
「言わないって約束するから」

トムは、ベッキーがその紙を引っぱるのにまかせた。ベッキーは、そこに書いてあることばを読んだ。「わたしはあなたを愛しています」

「まあ、いやあね！」ベッキーはトムの手を叩いた。でも顔はうれしそうだった。

するといきなり耳をつかまれ、椅子から引っぱりあげられるのを感じた。そして先生にいつもの席に戻された。みんなゲラゲラ笑っている。

トムの耳は痛かったけれど、心はうれしくて踊っていた。

# 7 A Plan is Made

At noon Tom ran to Becky and said quietly:

"Start to go home with the others, and then return here. I will do the same."

Soon both had returned. Alone in the school, Tom showed Becky how to make a picture of a house. He felt very happy.

He said, "Becky, were you ever engaged?"

"What does that mean?"

"Did you ever promise to marry any boy?"

"No."

"Would you like to be engaged?"

"What do you do?"

"You tell a boy that you will marry him. Then you kiss. That is all. It is easy."

"Why do you kiss?"

■engage 動 婚約する　■Would you like to ~ ? ～しませんか？

# 7. 計画は万全

　お昼の時間になると、トムはベッキーのところへ走っていき、こっそりと言った。
「他のみんなと家へ帰るふりをするんだ。それから、とちゅうで戻ってくるんだよ。ぼくも同じようにするからね」
　すぐに、ふたりは戻ってきた。学校にふたりきりで、トムはベッキーに家の絵の描き方を教えた。トムはうれしくてならなかった。
　トムは言った。「ベッキー、婚約したことある？」
「それって、どういう意味？」
「だれかと結婚する約束をしたかい？」
「してないわ」
「婚約したいと思わないかい？」
「どんなふうにするの？」
「男の子に、わたしはあなたと結婚しますって言うんだ。それからキスをする。それだけさ。簡単だろ」
「なんでキスするの？」

## 7. A Plan is Made

"They always do that. Do you remember what I was writing?"

"Yes."

"What was it? Shall I tell you?"

"Yes—but not now. Tomorrow."

"No. Now." He put his arm around her and said the words quietly. "Now you tell me."

She made him turn his face away as she said, "I—love—you!"

Tom kissed her and said, "Now it is all finished, Becky. And always after this you can only love me and can only marry me."

"And you can't marry any girl but me."

"Of course. That is part of it. And we will walk to school together. Because we are engaged."

"It is nice. I never heard of it before."

"Oh, it is good. Me and Amy Lawrence—"

Her big eyes told him that he had said the wrong thing.

■shall 助《疑問文で》〜しましょうか　■any 〜 but …以外の〜

## 7. 計画は万全

「そうするって決まってるからさ。ぼくが書いてたこと、覚えてる?」

「覚えてるわ」
「なんて書いてあった? ぼくが言おうか?」
「うん——でも、いまはいやよ。明日ね」
「だめだ。今だよ」トムはベッキーの体に腕をまわし、そのことばを、そっとささやいた。「さあ、今度はベッキーが言うんだよ」
　ベッキーは、トムの顔を向こうに向けながら言った。「わたしは——あなたを——愛しています!」
　トムはベッキーにキスをして言った。「さあ、これですんだよ、ベッキー。これからはいつだって、ぼくしか好きになっちゃいけないし、ぼくとしか結婚しちゃいけないんだよ」
「そしてトムは、あたし以外の女の子と結婚しちゃいけないのね」
「もちろんさ。そういうことでもある。それに、学校も一緒に歩いていくんだ。だって、婚約したんだから」
「まあ、すてきね。そんなこと、聞いたことなかったわ」
「うん、すてきだろう。ぼくとエイミー・ローレンスが——」
　ベッキーの大きく見開いた目を見て、トムはまずいことを言ったと気づいた。

## 7. A Plan is Made

"Oh, Tom! I am not the first girl that you were engaged to!" She began to cry.

"I do not love her now. I only love you."

More crying.

Tom took his favorite thing from his pocket. It was a gold-colored ball.

"Becky, take this."

She hit it from his hand to the floor.

Tom was angry and walked out of the school, and into the hills. He did not return.

Becky had not really wanted him to go, and when he did not return, she called, "Tom! Come back!" and cried again.

■ want someone to (人に)〜してほしい

## 7. 計画は万全

「まあ、トムったら！ 婚約したのは、あたしが初めてじゃなかったのね！」
ベッキーは泣きだした。
「エイミーのことは、もう好きじゃないよ。好きなのはベッキーだけだよ」
ベッキーの泣き声は大きくなるばかり。
トムはポケットからいちばんお気に入りのおもちゃを取り出した。それは金色のボールだった。
「ベッキー、これをあげるから」
ところがベッキーは、そのボールをトムの手から床にはたきおとした。
トムは腹を立てて、学校から歩いて出ていき、丘に登っていった。そしてもう学校には戻らなかった。
ベッキーは、ほんとうはトムに行ってほしくなかった。トムが帰ってこないので、「トム！ 帰ってきてよ！」と呼びながら、また泣きだした。

# 8 Tom Decides What to Do

Half an hour later Tom was sitting under a tree in the forest. He was very sad. He wished he could die—for a short time.

But soon he began to think of living again. He would travel to many countries. How would Becky feel then? He would become famous. Or he would join the Indians. But no, there was something better. He would be a pirate and steal gold from other ships. Tom Sawyer the Pirate!

Yes, it was decided. He would start the next morning.

Suddenly he heard a call from far away in the forest.

Now he was not Tom Sawyer. He was Robin Hood.

Moving slowly he called, "Stay where you are. Do not move until I call."

He saw Joe Harper. Tom called, "Stop! Who comes here into Sherwood Forest? No person enters my forest until I say that he may!"

■think of 〜のことを考える　■pirate 名海賊　■steal 動盗む　■may 助〜してもよい

## 8. トム、心を決める

　半時間後、トムは森の中で木の下にすわっていた。とても悲しかった。死にたいくらいだった——ほんのしばらくのあいだでいいから。
　でもすぐに、トムはまた生きることを考えだした。いろんな国をいっぱい旅するんだ。そしたら、ベッキーはどう思うだろう？　おれは有名になる。インディアンになってもいいな。いや、だめだ、もっといいことがある。海賊になって、他の船から金貨を奪うんだ。海賊トム・ソーヤーだ！

　そうだ、決めたぞ。明日の朝から出発だ。
　そのとたん、森の遠くのほうからラッパの音が聞こえた。
　こうくると、いまのおれはトム・ソーヤーじゃない。ロビン・フッドだ。
　ゆっくりと進みながら、トムは呼びかけた。「みなの者、その場で待て。呼ぶまで動くでないぞ」
　あらわれたのは、ジョー・ハーパーだった。トムは大声で言った。「とどまれ！　ここシャーウッドの森に入ってくるとは、いったい何者だ？　なんびとも、ことわりもなく我が森に入ることは許さんぞ！」

## 8. Tom Decides What to Do

"I am Guy of Guisborne," said Joe Harper, continuing the game. "I go where I want. Who are you?"

"I am Robin Hood. Soon you will be dead."

"Are you really that famous man? I am happy to fight you."

They began a slow and careful fight. Then Tom said, "Now fight faster."

Soon they were tired. "Fall!" Tom said. "You must fall!"

"You fall! I am fighting better than you."

"But the story of Robin Hood says that I kill you. Turn and let me hit you in the back."

Joe turned, was hit and fell.

"Now," Joe said, rising, "You must let me kill you."

"I can't do that. It is not in the story."

"It should be."

"OK, Joe, you can be Robin, and you can kill me."

Joe agreed, and more fighting followed.

When the boys went home, they were sad because Robin Hood had lived so long ago. They would have liked living with him in Sherwood Forest better than being President of the United States.

■would have done 〜したであろう　■President 图 大統領

## 8. トム、心を決める

「おれさまは、ギズボーンのガイだ」とジョー・ハーパーは言って、ロビン・フッドごっこを続けた。「おれさまは自分の行きたいところへ行くのさ。きさまこそ何者だ？」

「われこそはロビン・フッド。おまえの命はもうないと思え」

「ほんとに、あの有名なロビン・フッドか？ では、喜んで相手になってやろう」

ふたりはゆっくり、慎重に戦いだした。それからトムが、「さあ、もっと早くやろうぜ」と言った。

しばらくすると、ふたりとも疲れてきた。「倒れろよ！」とトムが言った。「おまえが倒れなきゃいけないんだぞ！」

「おまえが倒れろよ！ おれのほうが勝ってるじゃないか」

「でもロビン・フッドの本には、ロビンがガイを殺すって書いてあるんだぞ。後ろを向けよ、おれが背中を切りつけるから」

ジョーは後ろを向き、背中を切られて倒れた。

「さあ」と、ジョーは立ち上がりながら言った。「今度はおまえがやられる番だぞ」

「そんなことできないよ。本に書いてないだろ」

「ずるいぞ」

「わかったよ、ジョー、おまえがロビンになれよ、そしたら、おれを殺せるから」

ジョーが納得したので、それからさらに戦いが続いた。

戦い終えて家に帰るとき、ロビン・フッドがずっと昔の人だということを考えて、ふたりは悲しくなった。シャーウッドの森でロビン・フッドとすごせるなら、アメリカ合衆国の大統領になるよりいいと思うのだった。

## 覚えておきたい英語表現

> He didn't stop painting. （p.20, 3行目）
> 彼は塗るのをやめなかった。
>
> then stopped to look at his work. （p.20, 12行目）
> そして（トムは）作業をとめて自分の仕事のできばえを眺めた。

【解説】高校で必ず習う表現ですね。

① stop Ving： Vするのをやめる（中止する）
② stop to V： Vするために立ち止まる（手をとめる）

　似ている上にまったく意味が異なるので紛らわしい表現です。to Vは不定詞の副詞的用法なので、「Vするために」と理解すればよいのですが、ここではVingとto Vの持つイメージから理解を深めてみましょう。

　まずVingですが、これは現在分詞です。色々な場面で使われますが代表的なものが現在進行形です。"He is running."「彼は（今）走っています」のようにVingは**目の前で行われている**様子を表します。彼は走っている最中ですから、既にその動作は行われていると理解できます。Vingは「現在から過去」の時間軸を意識させる言葉なのです。よって"He stopped smoking."は「彼が既にタバコを吸っていて、それをstopした」と理解できます。

　それに対してto Vは未来志向の表現です。私はよく「toは"矢印"のイメージだよ!」と生徒に教えています。前置詞toと不定詞to（副詞的用法）を"→"で置き換えてみましょう。

【例文】
I went to a theater to watch the movie.
僕はその映画を見るために映画館へ行った。

I went 　→ 　a theater 　→ 　watch the movie.
私行った 　→ 　映画館に 　→ 　映画見る（見た）

　よってHe stopped to smoke. はHe stopped（彼は止まった）→ smoke（タバコを吸った）となるので「彼はタバコを吸うために立ち止まった」という意味になります。

Ving は「過去志向」、to V は「未来志向」と覚えておくと次のような表現も簡単に理解できます。

【例文】

> Please remember going to the party.
> あのパーティーに行ったことを忘れないでね。
>
> Please remember to go to the party.
> 忘れずにそのパーティーに行ってね。

---

> Now they knew they had been silly. （p.34, 14行目）
> 今彼らは自分たちが愚かだったことを悟った。

---

【解説】過去完了形は「had＋動詞の過去分詞形（Vpp）」で表現します。上の文では"had been"がそれです。日本語にはない文法なので苦手に感じる方が多いようです。
　"I bought a watch. I lost my watch."と誰かが言ったとします。これだと「買った時計を失くしたの?」「時計を失くしたから新しいものを買ったの?」という2通りの解釈がありえます。しかし次の文のように……

【例文】

> I lost my watch which my father had bought me 10 years ago.
> 父が10年前に買ってくれた腕時計を失くしてしまった。

　過去完了形を用いることで、「買ってくれた（had bought）時計を → 失くした（lost）」という時系列になっていることが文法的に明示されているわけです。

　本文に戻りましょう。子どもたちが気づいた（knew）のは「過去」の時点。「愚かだった」（チケットをトムに売ったこと）のは、それよりも前の出来事ですから過去完了形の"had been silly"で表現している文です。
　英語はとても論理的な言語です。文法的に時系列をはっきりさせることで、出来事の順番を相手に誤解なく伝えられるのです。

# Scene 2

# 9 Indian Joe Explains

At nine that night Tom and Sid were sent to bed as always. They prayed, and Sid quickly went to sleep. Tom was waiting.

Time passed very slowly and soon Tom was asleep. In his dreams he heard a cat call. Then a neighbor opened a window. Tom heard this, and quickly jumped out of his window making a sound like a cat. Huckleberry Finn was there with his dead cat.

In half an hour the boys were in the graveyard.

It was on a hill near the village. Tom was afraid that the sound of the wind came from the spirits of the dead. The boys found the new grave and sat down under a tree near it.

"Huck, do you believe that the dead people are pleased to have us here?"

"I wish I knew."

"Huck, do you think Williams hears us talking?"

"His spirit hears us."

■graveyard 名 (教会そばの) 墓地　■spirit 名 霊魂　■grave 名 墓　■be pleased to 〜
してうれしい

## 9. インジャン・ジョー、話をでっちあげる

　その夜、9時になると、トムとシッドはいつものように寝室へ行かされた。ふたりはお祈りをして、シッドはすぐ眠りについた。でもトムはじっと待っていた。
　時間はなかなか進まず、そのうちトムは寝入ってしまった。夢の中で、ネコの鳴き声が聞こえた。すると近所の人が窓を開けた。それを聞きつけたトムは、あわててネコの鳴きまねをしながら窓から飛びだした。ハックルベリー・フィンが、死んだネコを持って立っていた。
　半時間後、ふたりは墓地にいた。
　墓地は村のそばの丘の上にあった。風の音がすると、死人の声じゃないかとトムは不安になった。ふたりは新しい墓を見つけて、そのそばの木の下にすわった。
　「ハック、死んだ人たちは、おれたちがここにいても、いやがらないかな？」

　「そんなこと、おいら、わかんないよ」
　「ハック、ウィリアムズがおれたちの話を聞いてると思う？」
　「やつの魂が聞いてるだろうな」

## 9. Indian Joe Explains

Tom touched Huck's arm. "Did you hear it? There it is again! Now you hear it."

The two boys were afraid and held each other close.

"Tom, they are coming! What shall we do?"

"I don't know. Will they see us?"

"Tom, they can see in the dark, like cats. I wish I had not come."

"Oh, don't be afraid. We are doing nothing. If we are quiet, they won't see us."

"I will try, Tom. But I am afraid."

"Listen!"

The sound of voices got closer.

"Look! See there!" said Tom. "What is it?"

"They are devils. Oh, Tom, this is very bad."

Some voices came very near, carrying a light. The boys were very afraid. "It is the devils. Three of them. We are in great trouble Tom. Can you pray?"

"I will try." Tom began to pray.

"Tom! They are human! That is old Muff Potter's voice. He is drunk, as always. He won't see us."

"Huck, I know another voice. It is Indian Joe."

■drunk 形 酔っ払った

## 9. インジャン・ジョー、話をでっちあげる

　トムがハックの腕にさわった。「おい聞いたか？　ほら、またた！　今度は聞こえるだろ」
　ふたりの少年はこわくなって、体を寄せあった。
　「トム、こっちへ来るぞ！　どうしよう？」
　「わかんないよ。おれたちが見えるかな？」
　「トム、幽霊は暗やみでも見えるんだよ、ネコみたいにさ。ああ、来なきゃよかったな」
　「おい、こわがるなよ。おれたち、何もしてないじゃないか。静かにしてれば、やつらには見えないさ」
　「やってみるよ、トム。でも、おっかないなあ」
　「しっ、聞けよ！」
　声がさらに近づいてきた。
　「見ろよ！　ほら、あそこ！」とトム。「あれは何だ？」
　「悪魔だ。おいトム、こいつは、ほんとにやばいぞ」
　何人かの声が、明かりとともに、すぐそばまで近づいた。ふたりは、こわくてたまらなかった。「悪魔だよ。3人もいる。ほんとに困ったな、トム。お祈りはできるか？」
　「やってみるよ」トムは祈りだした。
　「おいトム！　あいつら人間だ！　あれはマフ・ポッターじいさんの声だぜ。いつもみたいに酔っぱらってる。おいらたちに気づきやしないよ」
　「ハック、もうひとりの声も知ってるよ。インジャン・ジョーだ」

## 9. Indian Joe Explains

"Why are they here?"

Then the boys were quiet because the three men had arrived at the new grave. "Here it is," said the third voice. The boys saw the face of young Doctor Robinson.

"Be quick," he said.

The other two men began opening the grave. It was very quiet. They opened the box and took out the body. Potter had a knife. "Now, Doctor, it is ready. But you must give us five dollars more."

"You have your money," the doctor said.

"No, you must give us more," Indian Joe said.

The doctor hit him suddenly, and Indian Joe fell.

Potter dropped his knife. "You hit my friend," he said and began fighting with the doctor.

Indian Joe stood up and picked up Potter's knife. He waited for a chance to stab the doctor. Suddenly the doctor hit Potter, who fell to the ground.

Indian Joe saw his chance and stabbed the doctor. The doctor fell to the ground. And the two boys ran away.

Slowly the doctor died. Indian Joe put the knife in Potter's right hand and then waited for him to wake up.

■grave 名墓 ■body 名肉体、遺体 ■stab 動突き刺す

## 9. インジャン・ジョー、話をでっちあげる

「なんで、こんなところにいるんだ？」

やがて3人の男たちが、新しい墓のところまで来たので、少年たちは口をつぐんだ。「ここだ」と、3人目の男が言った。年若いロビンソン医師の顔が見えた。

「早くしろ」と医者は言った。

他のふたりが墓をあばきはじめた。あたりは、しいんと静まりかえっている。男たちは棺のふたを開け、死体を取り出した。ポッターはナイフを持っていた。「さあ、お医者さまよ、準備できたぜ。だけど、おれたちにもう5ドルよこしな」

「金はもう払っただろう」と医者が言った。

「だめだ。もっとよこすんだ」とインジャン・ジョーが言う。

医者がいきなり殴りかかったので、インジャン・ジョーは地面に倒れた。

ポッターはナイフを落とすと、「おれの相棒を殴ったな」と言って、医者と殴り合いになった。

インジャン・ジョーが立ち上がって、ポッターのナイフを拾った。そして医者を刺す機会をうかがった。そのとたん医者がポッターを殴り、ポッターは倒れて気を失った。

インジャン・ジョーはその機会をとらえて、医者をナイフで刺した。医者は、どうと地面に倒れた。ふたりの少年は、あたふたと走って逃げた。

ゆっくりと医者は死んでいった。インジャン・ジョーはナイフをポッターの右手に握らせて、気がつくのを待った。

## 9. Indian Joe Explains

Soon Potter began to move. He saw the knife in his hand. Then he saw the doctor's body. "What happened, Joe?" he said.

"It is bad," said Joe. "Why did you do it?"

"I didn't do it!" Potter was afraid. "I was drunk. I don't remember. Did I do it, Joe? I never wanted to do it."

"He hit you and then you did it. But you are a good friend, Muff Potter. I won't tell anyone."

"Oh, Joe, thank you." And Potter began to cry.

"There is no time to cry. We must leave quickly. Move, now."

Potter started running. Joe watched him. "He forgot his knife because he is drunk. When he remembers, he will be afraid to return for it." Joe left.

The dead doctor, the body and the opened box were alone in the graveyard.

## 9. インジャン・ジョー、話をでっちあげる

　やがてポッターが身動きしだした。そして自分の手にあるナイフを見た。それから医者の死体に目をやった。「何があったんだ、ジョー？」とポッターは言った。
　「まずいな」とジョー。「なんで、こんなことをやらかしたんだ？」
　「おれはやってない！」ポッターはこわくなった。「酔っぱらってたんだ。覚えてねえよ。おれがやったのか、ジョー？ そんなつもりは全然なかったんだ」
　「あいつがおまえを殴って、それでおまえが刺したんだ。でもおまえは親友だ、マフ・ポッター。だれにも言いやしねえよ」
　「そうか、ジョー、ありがとうよ」そしてポッターは泣きだした。
　「泣いてる暇はねえぜ。さっさと、ずらからねえと。さあ、行け」

　ポッターは走りだした。ジョーはその後ろ姿を見つめていた。「酔ってるから、ナイフを忘れて行きやがった。思い出しても、こわくて取りに来れないだろうぜ」そしてジョーも立ち去った。
　死んだ医者と、掘り出された死体、そして開いた棺だけが墓場に残された。

# 10 The Promise
## —The Boys are Afraid

The two boys were very afraid. They ran to the village and into an old, empty building.

"Huckleberry, what will happen now?"

"If the doctor dies, they will hang Indian Joe."

Tom spoke. "But who will tell about it? You and I?"

"If we tell and Indian Joe does not die, he will kill us. Maybe Muff Potter will tell what happened. He is usually drunk."

Tom said, "Muff Potter does not know what happened. The doctor hit him. Huck, are you sure that you won't tell?"

"Tom, we can't tell. Indian Joe would kill us like two cats if we told. Tom, we must never tell. We must make a promise. In writing."

■hang 動 〜を絞首刑にする、吊るす　■make a promise 約束をする

## 10. 誓い──少年たち、おびえる

　ふたりの少年は、こわくてたまらなかった。村まで走っていき、古い空き家に入った。
「ハックルベリー、これからどうなるんだ？」
「あの医者が死んだら、インジャン・ジョーはしばり首だな」
　トムは言った。「だけど、だれがそれを知らせるんだ？ おまえとおれか？」
「もし、おいらたちが知らせて、それでもインジャン・ジョーが死ななかったら、おいらたちを殺しにくるよ。たぶん、マフ・ポッターが、何があったか話しちまうだろうさ。いつも酔っぱらってんだから」
　トムは言った。「マフ・ポッターは何があったか知らないじゃないか。医者に殴られて気を失ってたんだから。ハック、おまえ、ほんとうにしゃべらないな？」
「トム、おいらたち、しゃべれないぜ。もしだれかに言ったら、インジャン・ジョーはおいらたちを、2匹のネコみたいに簡単に殺しちまうぜ。トム、ぜったいだれにも言っちゃだめだ。誓いを立てなくちゃな。ちゃんと誓約書を書いてさ」

## 10. The Promise—The Boys are Afraid

Tom agreed. On a piece of wood he wrote:

*Huck Finn and Tom Sawyer promise they will never tell about this, and they wish they may die if they ever tell.*

Then each boy cut a finger and signed in blood, TS and HF. Tom helped Huck to write his H and F.

Then they put the piece of wood in the ground.

Tom entered his house through his bedroom window. It was almost morning. He went to bed quietly, thinking that his aunt would never know. But Sid was not sleeping.

The next morning his aunt gave him some food. Then she cried, and asked why he couldn't be good. She wanted him to be good, but she couldn't help any more.

Tom also cried and promised to be good. But he felt that she did not believe him.

He went to school, where the teacher hit him and Joe Harper because they had run away from school the day before.

Then he went to his seat. On his chair was the bright, gold-like ball that he had given to Becky Thatcher. Now his heart was broken.

■may 助 ～してもかまわない　■if someone ever もし[万が一]～なら　■day before 前の日

## 10. 誓い——少年たち、おびえる

　トムは賛成した。そして1枚の板切れに、こう書いた。

　　ハック・フィンとトム・ソーヤーは、このことを、けっしてだれにも
　　言いません。もしだれかに言ったら、死んでもかまいません。

それから、それぞれ指を切って、血でサインをした。トム・ソーヤーの頭文字のＴＳと、ハックルベリー・フィンの頭文字のＨＦだ。トムは、ハックがＨとＦの字を書くのを助けてやった。
　そしてふたりはその板切れを土の中に埋めた。
　トムは寝室の窓から家の中へ入った。もうほとんど朝だった。トムはそっとベッドにもぐりこみながら、おばさんには気づかれないだろうと思った。ところが、シッドが眠っていなかったのだ。
　翌朝、おばさんは朝食を出してくれた。でもそのあと泣きだして、どうしていい子になれないの、とトムに言った。いい子になってもらいたいのに、もう、おばさんの手には負えないと言う。
　トムも泣きだして、いい子になるよ、と約束した。でも、おばさんは信じてくれないようだった。
　学校へ行くと、先生がトムとジョー・ハーパーをムチで叩いた。まえの日に学校を抜けだしたからだ。
　それから席についた。すると椅子の上に、きらきらした金色のボールがあった。ベッキー・サッチャーにあげたものだ。いまやトムの心は、すっかりうちのめされてしまった。

# 11 Tom is Worried

Soon everyone knew the bad news about the doctor and the teacher closed the school.

Potter's knife had been found. Someone saw Potter washing in a small river, in the early morning. This was strange because Potter never washed.

All the people in the town were slowly going toward the graveyard. Tom and Huckleberry went too, but they did not want to go. Tom was afraid when he saw the grave again and very afraid when he saw Indian Joe.

Then Muff Potter went to the grave. Some people saw him and shouted. He was with a policeman. Potter looked afraid when he saw the dead doctor and began to cry.

"I did not do it, friends," he said. "I did not do it."

"Who said that you did?" a voice shouted.

Potter saw Indian Joe, and said:

"Oh, Indian Joe, you promised me that you would never—"

"Is this your knife?" the policeman asked.

Potter fell to the ground.

■worried 形 心配した　■fall to the ground 地面に落ちる

# 11. トム、心配する

　やがて、医者が殺されたという悪いニュースがみんなに知れわたり、先生は学校をお休みにした。
　ポッターのナイフが見つかった。さらに早朝、ポッターが小川で体を洗っているのを見た人がいた。ポッターはぜったい体を洗ったりしないので、これはあやしかった。
　町じゅうの人が、ゆっくりと墓地へ向かった。トムとハックルベリーもついていったが、ほんとうは行きたくなかった。あの墓をもういちど見て、トムはこわくなった。さらにインジャン・ジョーを見かけて、もっとこわくなった。
　そのときマフ・ポッターが墓場にやってきた。何人かがポッターを見て、悲鳴をあげた。ポッターは警官と一緒だった。ポッターは医者の死体を見ると、おびえるような顔をして泣きだした。
　「おれがやったんじゃねえよ、なあ、みんな」とポッターは言った。「おれじゃねえ」
　「おまえがやったと、だれが言ったんだ？」と叫ぶ声がした。
　ポッターはインジャン・ジョーの顔を見て、言った。
　「くそ、インジャン・ジョー、ぜったい言わないって、約束したじゃねえか——」
　「これはおまえのナイフか？」と警官が聞いた。
　ポッターは地面にくずおれた。

## 11. Tom is Worried

"Tell them, Joe. Tell them."

Indian Joe told his story.

Huckleberry and Tom stood still and were not able to speak.

They wished to tell the true story, but were too afraid.

For a week Tom could not sleep well. One morning Sid said, "Tom, you talk in your sleep so much that I can't sleep."

Tom's face became white and he looked away. "This is bad," said Aunt Polly. "What is wrong, Tom?"

"Nothing," he answered.

"And you say bad things!" Sid said. "Last night you said, 'He's dead! He's dead!' Then you said, 'Do not hurt me. I will not tell!' Tell what?"

Aunt Polly said, "I understand. It is about the doctor. I dream about it too."

Mary said that she also dreamed about it, and then Sid stopped talking.

Slowly Tom could sleep easier.

Almost every day, Tom went to the prison window and gave Potter some small present. Then he felt happier.

The village people wanted to put Indian Joe in prison too. Like Muff Potter, he had been helping the doctor to carry away the dead body from the grave. But the people did nothing. Everyone was afraid of Indian Joe.

■stand still じっと立っている　■prison 图牢屋、拘置所　■carry away 持ち去る
■be afraid of 〜を恐れる

## 11. トム、心配する

「言えよ、ジョー。言ってくれ」
インジャン・ジョーは、自分の作り話を言ってきかせた。
ハックルベリーとトムは、じっと立ったまま、何も言えなかった。

ふたりはほんとうのことを話したかったが、こわくてできなかった。
それから1週間、トムはよく眠れなかった。ある朝シッドが言った。「トム、寝言がうるさくって、眠れないよ」
トムの顔は真っ青になり、目をそらした。
「おや、それはよくないね」とポリーおばさん。「どうかしたの、トム?」
「なんでもないよ」とトムは答えた。
「それに、よくないことばっかり言うんだよ!」とシッドが言った。「昨日の夜なんか、『死んでる!死んでる!』なんて言ってたよ。それから、『殺さないでくれ。だれにも言わないから!』だって。いったい、何を言わないの?」
ポリーおばさんが言った。「ああ、わかった。お医者さまの事件だね。あたしもよく夢に見るよ」
メアリーも、その事件の夢を見ると言ったので、シッドは話すのをやめた。

時がたつと、しだいにトムはぐっすり眠れるようになった。
ほとんど毎日、トムは牢屋の窓のところへ行って、ポッターに少しばかりのプレゼントを渡した。そうすると、心が軽くなるのだった。
村の人たちは、インジャン・ジョーも牢屋に入れたいと思っていた。マフ・ポッターと同じように、医者が墓から死体を盗むのを手伝っていたからだ。でも、人々は何もしようとしなかった。だれもがインジャン・ジョーを恐れていたのだ。

# 12 Tom is Kind

Tom had a new problem. Becky Thatcher was sick. He was worried that she would die.

He was sad. He did not play games. He was not interested in anything.

His aunt did not know what was wrong and tried to help him.

She was always reading about health. She believed everything she read. When she read something new, she wanted to try it.

She took Tom outside in the early morning and threw cold water over him. Then she put him to bed. She thought that this would help him.

But Tom became sadder and sadder.

Next she tried hot water instead of cold. Then she tried less food. Then she heard of something new called Painkiller. She ate some. The taste was like fire.

■比較級 and 比較級　どんどん、ますます　■painkiller 名 痛み止め

# 12. トムはやさしい子

　トムに新しい心配ごとができた。ベッキー・サッチャーが病気になったのだ。ベッキーが死んでしまうのじゃないかと、トムは心配した。
　トムは悲しかった。ごっこ遊びもやらない。何をしても、おもしろいと思えなかった。
　おばさんは原因を知らないまま、なんとかトムを元気にしてやろうとしていた。
　おばさんはいつも、健康についての本を読んでいた。そして読んだものはなんでも信じた。何か新しいことが書いてあるのを読むと、すぐためしたくなるのだった。
　おばさんは朝早くにトムを外へつれだすと、冷たい水をぶっかけた。それからベッドに押しこんだ。これでトムが元気になると、おばさんは思ったのだ。

　でもトムはますます悲しげになり、しょんぼりするようになった。
　次におばさんは、冷たい水のかわりに、熱いお湯をぶっかけてみた。それから、ごはんをへらしてみた。さらに、「痛みどめ」という名の、何か新しいものを聞きつけてきた。おばさんはちょっと口にしてみた。すると口から火が出るほど辛かった。

## 12. Tom is Kind

She gave some to Tom and watched him. This Painkiller had a great result. The boy liked it very much. She knew that she had found the right thing.

Tom had some plans. First he said he liked Painkiller. He asked for it so often that his aunt gave him the full box. She did not know that every day he put some in a hole in the floor.

One day as he was doing this Peter, the cat, came in. Tom thought he wanted some of the Painkiller.

"You do not want it, Peter."

But Peter continued to ask for it.

"Are you sure?"

Peter was sure.

"You have asked for it, and I will give it to you. I am a kind boy. But if you do not like it, remember that you asked."

He gave the cat some Painkiller.

Peter jumped around the room and gave a loud cry. He went faster and faster around the room. Aunt Polly arrived as Peter jumped through the open window with a cry.

Tom was laughing a lot.

■so ~ that …なほど~  ■give a cry 大声を上げる

## 12. トムはやさしい子

　おばさんはトムにいくらか与えて、ようすを見た。この「痛みどめ」は、すばらしい効果を見せた。トムがとても気に入ったのだ。おばさんは、やっといいものを見つけたと思った。
　じつはトムには計画があった。まず、「痛みどめ」が気に入ったふりをする。そしてもっと欲しいと何度も言うと、おばさんは箱ごとトムにくれた。そして毎日、床の穴に落としていたのだが、もちろんおばさんは知らなかった。

　ある日、トムがまた床に落としていると、ネコのピーターが部屋に入ってきた。トムは、ピーターが「痛みどめ」を欲しがっているように思った。
「こんなの、欲しくないだろ、ピーター」
　でもピーターは、ねだりつづけた。
「ほんとか？」
　ピーターは本気らしい。
「おまえが欲しがるから、おれはやるんだぞ。おれはやさしい子だからな。もし気に入らなくても、自分が欲しがったことを忘れるなよ」
　トムはピーターに「痛みどめ」をやった。
　ピーターは部屋じゅうを跳びまわり、大声で鳴きわめいた。ますます速く、どんどん速く走りまわる。ポリーおばさんがあわててやってくると、ピーターはフギャーと鳴きながら、開いた窓から飛びだしていった。
　トムは笑いころげていた。

## 12. Tom is Kind

"Tom, what is wrong with the cat?"

"Cats always do that to show they are happy."

But Aunt Polly saw the Painkiller. She knew what had happened. She caught Tom's ear and pulled him up, then hit him with her hand. "Why did you do that to the cat?"

"Because I am sorry that he has no aunt to care for him."

"Has no aunt! Why do you say that?"

"Because if he had an aunt she would give him a drink that burned his mouth and not think of his feelings. She would say, if the drink was good for a human, it would be good for a cat."

Aunt Polly thought. If it hurt a cat, it would hurt a boy, also. She put her hand on Tom's head. "I was trying to help you."

"And I was trying to help Peter. And it helped him. I never saw him move so fast." He was smiling at her now.

"Oh, Tom! I will not give you any more Painkiller. Go to school. And try to be a good boy."

■What is wrong with ~? ~はどうかしたの？　■sorry 形気の毒に思って　■care for ~の世話をする　■burn 動 ~焼く、ヒリヒリさせる

## 12. トムはやさしい子

「トム、あのネコ、いったいどうしたの？」
「ネコってのは、うれしいときに、いつもああするんだよ」
 でもおばさんは「痛みどめ」に気がついた。そして何があったのかわかった。おばさんはトムの耳をつまんで上に引っぱりあげ、手で叩いた。「どうしてネコにそんなことしたの？」
「だって、ネコには世話を焼いてくれるおばさんがいなくて、かわいそうだと思ったんだよ」
「おばさんがいないって！ なんで、そんなこと言うの？」
「だって、もしネコにおばさんがいたら、舌が焼けそうに辛いものを飲ませるだろ。ネコがどう思うかなんて気にせずにね。人間にいいなら、ネコにもいいにちがいないって、ネコのおばさんは言うと思うよ」
 ポリーおばさんは考えこんだ。もしネコによくないなら、人間の子どもにもよくないにちがいない。おばさんはトムの頭に手をおいた。「おまえを元気にしてやろうと思ったんだよ」
「だから、ぼくはピーターを元気にしてやろうと思ったんだ。よく効いたよ。あんなに速く走るのを見たことないよ」トムはそう言いながら、いまではニヤニヤしていた。
「これ、トム！ もう『痛みどめ』はあげないよ。さあ、学校へ行きなさい。いい子にするんだよ」

## 12. Tom is Kind

Tom arrived early at school and waited at the gate. He did not play. He said he was sick.

Jeff Thatcher came down the road, and Tom's face was brighter. But quickly it was dark again. Jeff was alone.

When Tom saw a girl's dress from far away, he watched and watched. But the girl was never the right one.

Then one more dress came through the gate. Tom's heart jumped. Soon, he was outside again, shouting, laughing, running, standing on his head to make Becky Thatcher watch him.

She never looked at him. How could she not see him? He ran through a group of boys, and he fell at her feet.

She turned away with her nose in the air. "Some people always want other people to look at them!"

His face became red. He stood straight and walked quietly away.

■do and do 繰り返し〜する　■stand on one's head 逆立ちする　■turn away （体や顔を）背ける　■with nose in the air つんとそっぽを向いて

## 12. トムはやさしい子

　トムは早くに学校につき、校門のところで待っていた。友だちが来ても、具合が悪いのだと言い訳をして遊ばなかった。
　ジェフ・サッチャーが道を歩いてきたので、トムの顔は明るくなった。でもすぐに、また暗くなった。ジェフはひとりだったからだ。
　女の子の服が遠くから見えたとき、トムは目を細めて、じっと見つめた。でも、その女の子はめあての子ではなかった。
　そのとき、もうひとつの女の子の服が校門を通った。トムの胸はドキンとした。すぐにまた外へ出ていって、叫んだり、笑ったり、走ったり、逆立ちしたりして、ベッキー・サッチャーに見てもらおうとした。
　でもベッキーはトムを見ようとしなかった。どうして、こっちを見ないんだろう？　トムは男の子たちのあいだをすり抜けて走り、ベッキーの足元でころんだ。
　ベッキーは鼻をつんとあげて、そっぽを向いた。「いつも人に見てもらいたくて、目立つ子って、いるのよね！」
　トムの顔は真っ赤になった。そして、さっと立ち上がり、だまって歩き去った。

# 13 The Young Pirates

Tom had decided. He was a sad boy with no friends. No one loved him. He had tried to be good, but they would not let him. They were making him bad.

Far from the village he met his best friend, Joe Harper. Tom said that he was going to travel around the world, never to return to the village, and Joe wanted to go with him.

Joe's mother had hit him, even when he had done nothing. She must want him to go away, so he was going. He hoped she would be happy now and would never be sorry about sending her boy into the cold world to die.

The two boys walked together. They agreed to be like brothers until they died. They began to plan. They decided to be pirates.

They decided the island in the Mississippi River, near the village, would be a good place. The island was long, with many trees. No people lived on it.

They met Huckleberry Finn, and he joined them.

■plan 動計画を立てる

# 13. 小さな海賊たち

　トムの心は決まった。おれは友だちのいない、あわれな子どもだ。だれも愛してくれやしない。いい子になろうとしたのに、みんなそうさせてくれないんだ。みんなのせいで、悪い子になったんだ。
　村から遠く離れたところで、トムは親友のジョー・ハーパーに会った。トムが、これから世界じゅうを旅しに出て、もう村へは帰らないつもりだと言うと、ジョーも一緒に行きたがった。
　ジョーはお母さんにムチで叩かれたのだ。何も悪いことはしていないのに。お母さんはおれに出ていってもらいたいにちがいない。だから出ていくんだ。ジョーはいまでは、お母さんに幸せでいてほしいと思っていた。そして息子を冷たい世間へ追いやって死なせたことを、後悔して苦しまないでほしいと願った。
　ふたりの少年は一緒に歩いていった。死ぬまで兄弟同然だと誓いあった。そして計画を立てはじめた。ふたりは海賊になると決心したのだ。
　村のそばのミシシッピ川の中にある島が、ぴったりの場所だろうと話が決まった。島は縦に長くて、木がいっぱい生えていた。それにだれも住んでいない。
　ふたりはハックルベリー・フィンに出会い、仲間に入れた。

## 13. The Young Pirates

Each boy would find food and other useful things. Then they would meet at night by the river.

Tom arrived with meat and a few other things. He called two times. Then a voice said:

"Who goes there?"

"Tom Sawyer the Black Pirate. Name your names."

"Huck Finn the Red-Handed and Joe Harper the Destroyer of the Seas." Tom had taken these names from his favorite books.

"Speak the word."

Two voices spoke together: "Blood!"

Tom joined them.

Joe Seas had also brought meat, and Finn had cigarettes. The Black Pirate said that they must also have fire. They went to a large river-boat.

The boat-men were all in the village. Next to the river-boat was a raft. They took it and moved down the river.

After two hours their raft touched the island. They would sleep in the open air.

They built a fire and cooked some meat. It was wonderful to be eating in the forest, far from other people. They said that they would never return to a village again.

After eating, they sat on the ground. Huck smoked a cigarette.

■name 動 ～の名を挙げる ■raft 名 イカダ ■build a fire 火をおこす

## 13. 小さな海賊たち

　それぞれ食べ物や、他に必要なものを見つけてくることになった。そして夜になったら川のそばで集合だ。

　トムは、肉と、他にいくつか持って川についた。2度呼びかけた。すると、声がした。

「そこにいるのはだれだ？」

「『黒の海賊』トム・ソーヤーだ。名をなのれ」

「『血まみれ手』のハック・フィンに、『海の破壊者』ジョー・ハーパーだ」トムがこういう名前を、大好きな本から選んでおいたのだ。

「合いことばを言え」

　ふたりが声をそろえた。「血だ！」

　トムはふたりに加わった。

「海の破壊者」ジョーも肉を持ってきていて、フィンは巻きタバコを持ってきていた。「黒の海賊」が、火もいるじゃないか、と言った。みんなは大きな川船があるところへ行った。

　船頭たちはみんな村にいて、そこにはだれもいなかった。川船のとなりにイカダがつないである。子どもたちはそれを盗んで川を下った。

　2時間後、イカダが島についた。外で寝ることになりそうだ。

　3人は火をおこし、肉を焼いた。人々から遠くはなれ、森の中で食事するのは、最高の気分だった。もうぜったい村には帰らないぞ、とみんなが言った。

　食べ終わると、3人は地面にすわった。ハックはタバコを吸った。

## 13. The Young Pirates

Huck said, "What do pirates do?"

Tom said, "Oh, they enjoy life. They follow other ships and catch them and burn them. They take the money from those ships and put it in a deep hole in the ground on their island. And they kill the people on the ships."

"They carry the women to the island," said Joe. "They don't kill the women."

"No," Tom agreed. "Pirates are good. They don't kill the women. And the women are always beautiful."

"And their clothes are gold," said Joe.

"Whose clothes?" said Huck.

"The pirates'."

Huck looked at his clothes. "Then I am not dressed right," he said. "But these are my only clothes."

The other boys told him that the fine clothes would come later.

Slowly their talk ended. Huck went to sleep quickly. But the other boys could not sleep so quickly. They began to think. Had it been wrong to run away from home? Had it been wrong to take the meat? They decided that they would never take meat or other people's things again.

And with that decided, they also went to sleep.

■burn 動 〜を焼く　■run away 逃げだす

## 13. 小さな海賊たち

　ハックが言った。「海賊って、何をするんだ？」
　トムが言った。「そりゃあ、楽しいぜ。他の船を追いかけて、つかまえて、それから焼いてしまうんだ。その船から金を奪って、自分の島に掘った深い穴に隠すんだ。それから、船に乗ってたやつらを殺すのさ」

　「女は島につれていくんだ」とジョー。「海賊は女を殺さないのさ」

　「そうだ」とトムが応じた。「海賊はいいやつなんだ。女は殺さない。それに、女たちはいつだって美人なんだ」
　「それから、服は金ぴかだ」とジョー。
　「だれの服が？」とハック。
　「海賊さ」
　ハックは自分の服を見た。「じゃあ、おいらの格好はよくないな。でも、服はこれしかないんだ」
　他のふたりが、いい服はそのうち手に入るから、と言ってなぐさめた。

　しだいに、話すこともなくなってきた。ハックはさっさと寝入ってしまった。でもあとのふたりは、なかなか眠れなかった。いろいろ考えだしたのだ。家を逃げだすなんて、悪いことをしたかな？　肉を盗んだりして、やっぱりよくなかったかな？　もうこれからはぜったい、肉とか、人のものを盗まないようにしようと、ふたりは決心した。
　そう心に決めて、ふたりもやっと眠りにつくことができた。

# 14 Island Life
## —Tom Quietly Leaves

Opening his eyes, Tom forgot where he was. Then he remembered.

The forest was very quiet. Joe and Huck were still sleeping.

The life of the forest began to wake up. Birds started singing. Small animals moved in the trees.

Tom called to the others. Soon they were all playing in the river. Their raft had been carried away, but this pleased them. Now they were sure that they would never return to their village.

Happy and hungry, they built their fire. Huck had found some good water to drink. Joe cooked some meat. Tom and Huck went to the river to catch fish. The fish was very good. After that, they walked through the trees. The island was long and narrow. It was very near one river-bank, but far from the bank where the village was.

They played in the river often. In the afternoon they returned to their fire. They ate some meat again and talked.

■wake up 目を覚ます　■walk through 〜の中を通る　■river-bank 图川岸

# 14. 島の生活
## ——トム、こっそり抜けだす

　目を覚ましたとき、トムは自分がどこにいるのか忘れていた。それから、ああそうだったと思い出した。
　森はとても静かだった。ジョーとハックはまだ眠っている。
　森の生き物たちが目覚めだした。鳥が歌いだす。小さな動物たちが木の中でごそごそ動いている。
　トムは他のふたりに呼びかけた。しばらくすると、3人とも川で遊んでいた。イカダは流されてしまっていたが、みんなそれを喜んだ。これで、ぜったい村に帰らないという決心がついたのだ。

　うきうきしながら、そしておなかをすかせながら、みんなは火をおこした。ハックがきれいな飲み水を見つけてきた。ジョーが肉を焼いた。トムとハックが魚を釣りにいった。魚はびっくりするほどおいしかった。そのあと、みんなで森の中を探検した。島は縦に長く、幅はせまかった。片方の川岸にはとても近いけれど、村のあるほうの岸からはずいぶん離れていた。

　3人はしょっちゅう川で遊んだ。午後になると、たき火のところへ戻った。そしてまた肉を食べながら話した。

## 14. Island Life—Tom Quietly Leaves

But the talk soon stopped. They began to feel sad. Tom and Joe were thinking of home. Huck, who had no home, was thinking of the places where he usually went to sleep.

But they did not tell each other they felt sad.

Suddenly, they heard a sound. They looked at each other, and listened. Quiet—Bang! Then quiet, and then again, Bang!

"We must go and see."

They ran to the river near the town and looked across the water.

They saw a big river-boat. It was coming slowly down the river. There were many people on it. There were many small boats around it.

"I understand!" said Tom. "Someone has died in the river!"

"That is right," said Huck. "They did that last summer when Bill Turner died in the river. They look for the body when it rises to the top of the water."

"I wish that I was on that river-boat now," said Joe.

"Who do you think has died?" said Huck.

They listened and watched. Suddenly Tom said "Boys, I know! They are looking for us!"

■Bang! 图バン！（という音）■look for ～を探す

## 14. 島の生活——トム、こっそり抜けだす

　でも、話はすぐにとだえてしまった。だんだん寂しくなってきたのだ。トムとジョーは家のことを考えていた。ハックは帰る家がないので、いつもねぐらにしている場所のことを考えていた。
　でも自分が寂しがっていることを、お互い口には出さなかった。
　そのとたん、何かの音が聞こえた。3人は顔を見合わせ、聞き耳を立てた。しーんとして——バン！　また、しーんとしたと思うと、ふたたび、バン！
「見に行かなきゃ」
　3人は町に近いほうの川へ走っていき、流れの向こうに目をやった。

　大きな川船が見えた。ゆっくりと川を下ってくる。大勢の人が乗っている。まわりには小舟がたくさんついていた。

「わかった！」とトム。「だれかが川で死んだんだ！」
「うん、そうだ」とハック。「去年の夏、ビル・ターナーが川で死んだときも、あんなふうにしてたぜ。死体をさがしてるんだ。水面に浮いてこないか見てるのさ」
「あの川船に乗ってたらよかったのになあ」とジョー。
「なあ、だれが死んだんだと思う？」とハック。
　3人は聞き耳を立てながら、船を見つめた。いきなりトムが言った。「おい、わかったぞ！　みんな、おれたちをさがしてるんだ！」

## 14. Island Life—Tom Quietly Leaves

This was a wonderful thing to know. Everyone was looking for them. People were sorry that they had not always been kind to them. The town was talking about them. This was fine.

It was good to be a pirate.

That evening they ate more fish. Then they talked about what the village people were thinking and saying. Slowly they stopped talking and sat looking into the fire. Tom and Joe thought of people at home who may be sad. Joe began to speak of returning to the village.

Tom and Huck laughed at him.

Huck went to sleep. Then Joe went to sleep. Tom sat for a long time.

Then he stood up. He found two pieces of wood on which he could write. After writing on the wood, he put one piece in Joe's hat. He put the other in his pocket.

Then he ran quietly toward the river.

■look into 〜を見つめる

## 14. 島の生活——トム、こっそり抜けだす

　こりゃあ、すごいや、と3人は思った。みんなが、おれたちをさがしてる。やさしくしなかったことを、すまないと思ってるんだ。町じゅうが、おれたちの話でもちきりだ。こいつは、いいや。

　海賊になるのも、なかなかいいものだ。
　そのゆうべ、3人は魚をもっと食べた。食べながら、村の人たちはどう考えてるか、なんて言ってるかと話しあった。しだいに話がやんで、3人は火を見つめながらすわっていた。トムとジョーは、悲しんでいるかもしれない家の人たちのことを考えていた。ジョーが、村に帰ろうかと言いだした。

　トムとハックは、そんなジョーを笑って、からかった。
　ハックは眠りについた。そのあとジョーが寝入った。トムは長い間、ひとりですわっていた。
　それから、トムは立ち上がった。字が書けそうな板切れをさがし、2枚見つけた。板切れに何かを書くと、1枚をジョーの帽子の中に入れ、もう1枚は自分のポケットに押しこんだ。
　そして、こっそりと川に向かって走った。

# 15 Tom Learns What is Happening

A few minutes later Tom was walking through the water toward the bank. He sat in the small boat tied next to the river-boat. The river-boat began to move. He knew that this was the last time it would cross the river that night. Twelve minutes later the boat stopped. Tom got out and ran to the village.

Soon he was outside his aunt's house. He looked through a window into a room. There sat Aunt Polly, Sid, Mary, and Joe Harper's mother. They were talking. They were next to the bed, and the bed was between them and the door.

Tom went to the door and opened it quietly. He moved quickly across the room and under the bed. No one saw him.

"But," said Aunt Polly, "he was not bad. He was only full of life, like any young animal. He did not want to do bad things. And he was a very kind boy." She began to cry.

■bank 岸 ■get out 外へ出る ■full of life 元気いっぱいで

## 15. トム、村のようすを知る

　数分後、トムは川岸に向かって、流れの中を歩いていた。そして川船の横につながれた小舟にのりこんですわった。川船が動きだした。これがその夜、川を渡す最後の便だと、トムは知っていた。12分後、船がとまった。トムは抜けだすと、村へ向かって走った。

　しばらくすると、トムはおばさんの家の外に立っていた。そして窓から部屋の中をのぞきこんだ。ポリーおばさんと、シッド、メアリー、そしてジョー・ハーパーのお母さんがすわっていた。みんなで話している。その横にベッドがあって、ベッドはみんなとドアのあいだにおいてあった。
　トムはドアのところまで行き、そっと開けた。すばやく部屋を横切って、ベッドの下に隠れた。だれにも見られていない。
　「だけどね」とポリーおばさん。「悪い子じゃなかったんだよ。元気がよすぎただけでね。ほら、動物の子みたいにさ。悪いことがしたかったわけじゃないんだよ。それに、とってもやさしい子でねえ」おばさんは泣きだした。

## 15. Tom Learns What is Happening

"My Joe was the same. He was not really bad. And he was always kind. And now I shall never see him again!"

"I am sorry now for so many things! Only yesterday, the cat—" Crying, Aunt Polly told about the cat and the Painkiller. Tom was crying a little now. He could hear Mary crying too. Had he really always been a good boy? It was surprising. But now he was beginning to believe it. He wished to run to his aunt and make her happy. But he waited and listened.

Their raft had been found on the river. There was no hope. On Sunday everyone in the village would go to the church and pray for the boys.

Mrs. Harper went home. Sid and Mary went to bed. Then Aunt Polly prayed for Tom. Her words and her old voice were filled with love. Tom began to cry again.

Then she got into bed. It was a long time before she went to sleep.

Tom came out and looked at her. He loved her and he was very sorry for her. He took the piece of wood with his writing on it out of his pocket. He put it on a table. She would see it there in the morning.

■shall 助 必ず〜だろう ■only 副 つい、たった ■make someone happy （人を）喜ばせる ■get into 〜に入る

## 15. トム、村のようすを知る

「うちのジョーだって、おんなじですよ。ほんとは悪い子じゃないんです。いつだって、やさしかったしね。なのに、もう二度と会えないなんて！」

「すまなかったと思うことが、いっぱいあるんだよ！ つい昨日だって、ネコがね——」ポリーおばさんは泣きながら、ネコと「痛みどめ」の話をした。トムはちょっと泣けてきた。メアリーが泣いているのも聞こえる。おれって、ほんとにいつも、そんなにいい子だったかな？ びっくりだなあ。でもトムは、しだいにそのとおりだと思うようになった。いまにもおばさんに駆け寄って、喜ばせてあげたいと思った。でも、もう少し待って、話を聞くことにした。

子どもたちのイカダが川で見つかった。だからもう望みはない。日曜日には、村じゅうの人が教会へ行って、少年たちのために祈ることになっていた。

ハーパー夫人が家に帰った。シッドとメアリーは寝室に行った。そしてポリーおばさんがトムのために祈っていた。おばさんのお祈りと年老いた声は、愛情に満ちていた。トムはまた泣きだした。

そのあとおばさんはベッドに入った。でも眠りにつくまで、とても長い時間がかかった。

トムはベッドの下から出てきて、おばさんを見つめた。おばさんが好きだという思いがあふれてきて、とてもすまない気がした。トムはポケットから、字を書いた板切れを取り出した。それを机の上においた。朝になったら、おばさんが見るだろう。

## 15. Tom Learns What is Happening

But then a new thought came to him. He put the wood into his pocket again. Then he gave his aunt a kiss and left the house.

He ran to the river. He took a small boat and went back to the island.

Soon he was on the island. He heard Joe say:

"No. Tom is true, Huck. He will return. What do you think he has been doing?"

"Here I am!" cried Tom, stepping out from among the trees.

They ate fish while Tom told what he had been doing. Then Tom went to sleep until noon.

---

■Here I am. さあ来ましたよ。ここにいますよ。 ■step out 外へ出る

15. トム、村のようすを知る

　でもそのとき、新たな思いつきがトムの頭にひらめいた。板切れをまたポケットにしまった。そしておばさんにキスをすると、家をあとにした。

　トムは川に向かって走った。それから小舟に乗って島に戻った。

　やがて島についた。するとジョーの声が聞こえた。
「そんなことない。トムはウソなんかつかないよ、ハック。きっと戻ってくるさ。でも、何をしてるんだと思う？」
「おれなら、ここにいるぞ！」トムは声をはりあげながら、森の中から飛びだしていった。
　みんなで魚を食べながら、トムは自分が何をしていたか話した。それからトムは昼まで眠ることにした。

# 16 A Night Surprise

The boys played in the water. But the next day Joe was very sad. Would he ever be happy again? Huck also was sad. Tom was not happy, but he tried to look happy. He had something interesting to tell them, but he did not want to tell them yet.

He said, trying to look happy, "I think there have been pirates on this island before. Maybe they left an old box full of money? Shall we go and look for it."

But the other boys were not interested.

Joe said, "I want to go home. I am very sad here."

"Oh, no, Joe. You will feel better soon," said Tom. "Think of the good fishing here."

"I am not interested in fishing. I want to go home."

"But, Joe, this is the best swimming place."

"I don't want to swim. I want to go home."

"Baby! You want to see your mother."

■think of 〜のことを考えてみる

# 16. 夜のハプニング

　少年たちは川で遊んだ。でも次の日になると、ジョーはとても悲しくなった。また元気になれる日がくるのだろうか？　ハックもやっぱり悲しかった。トムも悲しかったが、元気そうに見せようとした。それに、ふたりに話すおもしろいことがあったのだが、いまはまだ話したくなかった。
　楽しそうなそぶりをしながら、トムは言った。「この島には昔、海賊がいたと思うな。もしかしたら、金貨でいっぱいの古い宝箱をおいてってるかもしれないぞ。さがしに行かないか」
　でも、あとのふたりの少年は興味を示さなかった。
　ジョーは言った。「家に帰りたいよ。ここにいたって、寂しいもん」
　「おい、おい、ジョー。そんなの、すぐによくなるよ」とトム。「考えてみろよ、ここなら魚だっていっぱい釣れるぜ」
　「釣りなんか、どうだっていいや。家に帰りたいんだ」
　「だけどさ、ジョー、ここくらい泳ぐのにいい場所はないぜ」
　「泳ぎたくなんてないよ。家に帰りたい」
　「この、赤ちゃん！　お母さんに会いたいんだろ！」

## 16. A Night Surprise

"Yes, I do want to see my mother. And you would want to see your mother if you had a mother. I am not a baby."

"But you like it here, Huck? You want to stay? You and I will stay?"

Huck said, "Y-e-s." He was not sure.

"Let Joe go, if he wants to go," Tom said.

"We do not need him."

Joe began to walk into the water to swim toward the village.

Tom looked at Huck. Huck looked away. Then Huck said, "I want to go, Tom. We can go, Tom, can't we?"

"I won't! You can go. But I am going to stay."

Huck started to walk sadly away. Tom wanted to follow. He hoped that they would stop, but they didn't. Suddenly Tom felt very sad and quiet.

He ran after the other boys, shouting, "Wait! Wait! I want to tell you something."

They stopped, and he ran toward them. They listened to him without an answering word or smile. As they began to understand they became happy and shouted.

■like it here ここが好きだ、この場所が気に入っている　■run after 〜を追いかける

## 16. 夜のハプニング

「そうさ、お母さんに会いたいんだ。おまえだって、お母さんがいたら会いたくなるさ。赤ちゃんなんかじゃないや」

「でも、おまえはここが好きだろ、ハック？ ここにいたいだろ？ おれとおまえは、ここにいるよな？」

ハックは言った。「う、うん」なんだか、はっきりしない。

「ジョーは行かせようぜ、行きたいんだったらさ」トムは言った。

「ジョーなんか、いなくたって平気だ」

ジョーは村に向かって泳ごうと、川に足を踏み入れて歩きだした。

トムはハックを見た。するとハックが目をそらした。そしてハックが言った。「おいらも行きたいな、トム。おいらたちも、行っていいだろ？」

「おれは行かないぞ！ おまえ行けよ。けど、おれはここに残るからな」

ハックは悲しそうに歩きだし、去っていった。トムもついていきたかった。ふたりが止まってくれたらいいのにと思ったけれど、止まってくれなかった。そのとたんトムはとても悲しくなり、なんだか、しーんとするのを感じた。

トムはふたりのあとを追いかけて叫んだ。「待てよ！ 待ってくれよ！ 話したいことがあるんだ」

ふたりが立ち止まると、トムはそこへ向かって走った。ふたりはトムの話を、返事もせず、にこりともしないまま聞いた。でもその内容がわかってくると、ふたりはうれしくなって、喜びの声をあげた。

## 16. A Night Surprise

That night, after eating, Tom wanted to learn to smoke. Joe wanted to try too. With Huck's help, they began.

Tom said, "This is easy. I could have learned long ago."

"This is nothing," said Joe. "I could do this all day. I don't feel sick."

Tom said, "I wish that the other boys could see us now. We won't tell them. And some time when they are with us, I will say, 'Joe, I want to smoke.' And you will say, 'My cigarettes are not very good.' And I will say, 'It does not need to be good if it is strong.'"

"That will be good, Tom! I wish we could do it now!"

"And we will tell them that we learned to smoke when we were pirates. And they will wish that they had been here!"

The talk continued for a short time, then stopped. Joe said, "I am going for a walk."

Tom said, "Let me go with you."

Huck sat down again and waited an hour. Then he was sad, and went to find his friends. Both were sleeping.

That night they did not talk much. When Huck began to smoke, they said no. Something they had eaten made them feel sick.

■feel sick 気持ちが悪い　■go for a walk 散歩に出かける

## 16. 夜のハプニング

　その夜の夕食後、トムはタバコを吸ってみたくなった。ジョーもやってみたかった。そこでハックに教えてもらって、ふたりは吸ってみた。

　トムは言った。「なんだ簡単じゃないか。もっと前から、吸ってりゃよかったな」

　「なんてことないな」とジョー。「一日じゅうだって吸ってられるよ。ちっとも気分悪くならないしさ」

　トムが言った。「他のみんなが、いまのおれたちを見てたらなあ。いや、みんなにはだまっとこう。そんでもって、いつか一緒にいるときに、おれが、『ジョー、タバコ吸いたいな』って言うんだ。そしたらおまえが、『おれのタバコは、あんまりよくないぜ』って言う。それでおれが、『よくなくてもいいさ、強いタバコならさ』って言うんだ」

　「そいつはいいや、トム！いまできたら、いいのにな！」

　「それから、海賊だったときにタバコを覚えたのさって言うんだ。あいつら、ここにいたらよかったのにって思うぜ！」

　話はしばらくのあいだ続いたが、やがてやんでしまった。ジョーが言った。「ちょっと散歩してくるよ」

　トムが言った。「おれも一緒に行く」

　ハックはすわり直し、1時間待った。やがて心細くなってきたので、ふたりをさがしに行った。すると、ふたりとも、ぐったりとして眠っていた。

　その夜はみんなあまりしゃべらなかった。ハックがまたタバコを吸いだしたが、ふたりはいらないと言った。何か口にしたもののせいで、気分が悪くなったというわけだ。

## 16. A Night Surprise

That night Joe opened his eyes and called to the other boys. The air was strange and heavy and hot. They were afraid. They sat together and waited.

A light filled the sky. Bright light. A loud sound. A cold wind. The light came and went away again, and the sound that followed became louder and louder. There was a strong wind and rain began to fall.

"Quick, boys, find a safe place," Tom shouted.

They ran to different places. Then heavy rain came down and they thought the island would be washed away.

But then the storm grew weaker and weaker and it became quiet again.

The boys saved their fire and cooked some meat on it.

In the morning, they all wanted to go home. Tom tried to find a new game to interest them.

He found one. Now they were Indians. Fighting Indians. But when the day ended, they smoked together, as Indians always did to show they were at peace. And two of them were happy it did not make them sick.

■come down（雨などが）降る　■wash away 洗い流す　■at peace 平和に

## 16. 夜のハプニング

　夜中にジョーが目を覚まし、他の少年たちを呼び起こした。大気がざわめき、重苦しく、蒸し暑かった。みんな、こわくなった。体を寄せあってすわり、嵐がすぎるのを待った。
　稲妻が空じゅうに広がった。まぶしい光。とどろく雷鳴。冷たい風。稲妻は近くで光ったかと思うと、また遠ざかり、それに続く雷鳴はどんどん大きくなっていく。強い風が吹いて、雨粒が落ちだした。

　「さあ、早く、安全なところへ行こう」とトムが叫んだ。
　3人は別の場所へ走っていった。すると激しい雨がふってきて、島が洗い流されるのではないかと思えるほどだった。
　でもそのうち、嵐はだんだんと弱まってきて、ふたたび静かになった。

　少年たちは火が消えないように守りながら、肉を焼いた。
　朝になると、みんな家に帰りたくなっていた。トムは、ふたりの気を引くような新しい遊びがないか、必死で考えた。
　遊びは見つかった。いまや少年たちはインディアンだった。戦うインディアンだ。でも日が暮れると、みんなは一緒にタバコを吸うことになった。インディアンは平和のしるしにいつもタバコを吸うからだ。そして、そのうちのふたりは、タバコを吸っても具合が悪くならなかったので、ほっとしていた。

## 覚えておきたい英語表現

> I wish *I knew.* （p.72, 下から3行目）
> そんなことわからないよ。
>
> I wish *I had not come.* （p.74, 6行目）
> 来なければよかったよ。

【解説】「I wish + 仮定法」で「〜だとよいのだが」という意味です。このように事実とは異なる願望などを述べる表現を仮定法といいます。現在の事実に反することを述べる時には仮定法過去形、過去の事実に反することは仮定法過去完了形を使います。文章にするとややこしく感じますが、例文で覚えると簡単です。斜線部分の時制に注目してください。

### 【仮定法過去形の例文】

I wish I \**were healthy*!
健康だったならなあ！（実際は健康ではない）

If only it *would* stop snowing.
雪がやんでくれたらなあ。（実際は降っている）

If I \**were* a bird, I *could* fly.
もし鳥なら飛べるのに。（実際は鳥ではないから飛べない）

\*仮定法過去形ではbe動詞はwasではなくwereになります。

### 【仮定法過去完了形の例文】

I wish she *hadn't told* him about Nick.
彼女が彼にニックのことを話さなかったらよかったのになあ。（実際は話した）

If I *had had* a time, I *could have shown* you around our town.
もし時間があったら、町を案内できたんですがね。（実際は案内できなかった）

本文の"I wish I knew."は直訳すると「知っていればよいのだが（つまり知らない）」、"I wish I had not come."は「来なければ良かったのだが（でも来てしまった）」という直訳になります。

『トム・ソーヤーの冒険』には仮定法がたくさん出てきます。英語マスターになるには

避けては通れない文法ですからぜひ慣れていただきたいと思います。

---

**Who *do you think* has died?** （p.104, 下から3行目）
誰が死んだんだと思う？

---

【解説】とても口語らしい表現なので取り上げました。もともとの文は "Who has died?"「誰が死んだんだ？」です。
　"Who has died?" は直接的に答えを聞いている表現です。答えを知らなければ "I don't know." で会話が終わってしまいますし、聞き方によっては詰問しているようにも感じます。do you think を付け加えることで相手の個人的な意見を聞くことになります、会話の相手をより意識したマイルドな印象の質問になります。

【例文】
　　Who *do you think* won the game?　　誰が試合に勝ったと思う？

　　What *do you think* is the right answer?　　正しい答えは何だと思う？

相手の意見としての答えを聞きたい時にぜひ使ってほしい表現です。

---

***as* Indians always did to show they were at peace**
（p.120, 下から3行目）
インディアンが平和を示すためにいつもするように

---

【解説】as S V で「S が V するのと同様に」という意味です。

【例文】
　　The boy did as his father did.
　　その少年は父親がしたようにやった。

　　He came back safely as he promised.
　　彼は約束した通り無事帰宅した。

## 覚えておきたい英語表現

　マーク・トウェインは自身も愛煙家であったため、『トム・ソーヤー』をはじめ彼の著作にはたくさん喫煙に関する詳細な記述が出てきます。彼の著作を通じて1800年代の喫煙文化を知ることができます。
　ちなみに同じアメリカ文学の巨人ヘミングウェイの短編シリーズ「ニック・アダムズ物語」の "Indian Camp" には、ネイティブ・アメリカンの陣痛に苦しむ女性のために、男性たちが外でタバコを吸い安産を祈っているシーンが出てきます。
さて、ここでマーク・トウェインのタバコに関する名言を紹介しておきましょう。

> "Giving up smoking is the easiest in the world.
> I know because I've done it thousands of times."

訳については……読者の皆様に任せることとしましょう。

# Scene 3

# 17 Tom's Plan Succeeds

But no-one was happy in the village that same afternoon. The village was quiet. Nobody spoke and children stopped playing.

Becky Thatcher was walking near the school. She thought, "Oh, I wish I had not returned the bright ball Tom gave me! I have nothing to help me remember him. He is gone now, and I shall never, never see him again."

She walked away crying.

A large group of boys and girls, friends of Tom's and Joe's, came to the school to look at the yard where they had played together. They spoke of things Tom and Joe had said and done. They tried to learn who was the last person to see the two boys. The children who were the last to talk with Tom and Joe felt very important.

One boy who also wanted to feel important said, "I had a fight with Tom Sawyer, and he was stronger than me."

■gone 形すでにない、死んだ ■never 副決して〜ない

# 17. トムの計画が成功する

　でもその同じ午後、村ではだれもが悲しんでいた。村じゅうが静まりかえっていた。話す人もいなければ、子どもたちも遊んでいなかった。

　ベッキー・サッチャーは学校のそばを歩いていた。ベッキーは思った。「ああ、トムがくれた、きらきらのボールを返さなきゃよかったわ！ トムを思い出せるようなものが何にもないんだもの。トムはもういない。あたしはもう二度と、けっしてトムに会えないんだわ」
　ベッキーは泣きながら歩いていった。
　大勢の子どもたち、トムやジョーの友だちが、一緒に遊んだ校庭を見ようと学校にやってきた。みんなは、トムやジョーがあんなことを言った、こんなことをしたと話しあった。そして、ふたりの少年に最後に会ったのはだれかなのか、調べようとした。トムやジョーと最後に話した子どもたちは、自分がとても重要人物になったような気がした。

　自分も重要人物になりたいと思って、ひとりの少年が言った。「ぼく、トム・ソーヤーとケンカしたことがあるよ。トムはぼくより強かったな」

## 17. Tom's Plan Succeeds

But most of the boys could say that.

The next morning everyone in the village went to the church. Outside the church they talked, but in the church they were very quiet.

The little church was full. Aunt Polly entered, followed by Sid and Mary and the Harper family. All were wearing black clothes. The other people in the church stood up, while the two families walked to the front of the church and sat down.

It was quiet again. They all prayed, and then sang a song. Now the church leader began to talk about the boys and how good they had been. People were sorry that they had thought these boys were bad. Everyone was crying.

Slowly the church door opened. One by one, everyone turned to look. Then everyone turned to look while the three dead boys walked to the front of the church. Tom was first, Joe next, and last came Huck. They had been listening to every word!

Aunt Polly, Mary, and the Harpers put their arms around Tom and Joe. Huck stood alone, not knowing what to do. He started to move away, but Tom stopped him and said:

■one by one ひとりずつ  ■put one's arms around 〜を抱きしめる

## 17. トムの計画が成功する

　でもそれは、ほとんどの少年たちに言えることだった。
　翌朝、村じゅうの人が教会へ向かった。教会の外では話し声がしたが、教会の中は静まりかえっていた。

　小さな教会は、人でいっぱいだった。ポリーおばさんが入ってきて、シッド、メアリー、そしてハーパー家の人たちがそれに続いた。みんな喪服を着ていた。教会にいる他の人たちが立ち上がり、その中をふたつの家族が教会の最前列に進んで席についた。
　また、しんと静かになった。みんなが祈りをささげ、讃美歌を歌った。そして牧師が少年たちについて、また、この子たちがどれほどいい子だったかについて話しだした。人々は、この少年たちを悪い子だと思ったりして、すまなかったと後悔した。だれもが泣いていた。
　ゆっくりと、教会の扉が開いた。ひとり、またひとり、そして全員が後ろをふり返った。みんなが後ろを見ると、なんと3人の死んだはずの少年たちが、教会の一番まえの席へ向かって歩いていくではないか。トムが先頭で、ジョーがその次、最後はハックだった。3人はずっと、みんなの話を聞いていたのだ！
　ポリーおばさん、メアリー、ハーパー家の人たちが、トムとジョーを抱きしめた。ハックはどうしていいかわからず、ひとりぼっちで立っていた。そして出ていこうとしたが、トムが引きとめて言った。

## 17. Tom's Plan Succeeds

"Aunt Polly, this is not right. Some person must be glad to see Huck."

"And some person shall be me. I am glad to see him, dear boy!" She put her arms around Huck too. And now Huck felt stranger than before.

"Sing! And sing your best!" cried the church leader.

Everyone was happy and sang loudly. It was the best church singing ever! Tom Sawyer knew that this was the best time in his life.

■dear 形 いとしい、大切な

## 17. トムの計画が成功する

「ポリーおばさん、こんなのよくないよ。だれかがハックに会えたことも喜んであげなくちゃ」

「そのだれかは、あたしだよ。もちろん会えてうれしいよ、ねえ、ハック！」

おばさんはハックのことも抱きしめた。抱きしめられたハックのほうは、こんな変な気もちになるのは初めてだった。

「さあ、歌いましょう！ 精いっぱい、歌いましょう！」と牧師が叫んだ。

みんなうれしくなって、大声で歌った。いままで教会で歌われた中で、最高の歌声だった！ トム・ソーヤーは、これこそ人生で最高のときだと思った。

# 18 Tom's Wonderful Dream

That was Tom's great plan—to return home with the other boys and go to the church to hear people praying for them. They had crossed the river at night and sat in the forest until morning. They went to sleep in the church until the people came. Then they appeared at the most important time.

The next morning, Aunt Polly and Mary were very loving to Tom. He had everything that he wanted to eat. They talked a lot. Aunt Polly said:

"We can laugh now, Tom. But you were not kind to let me worry. You came across the river to surprise us in the church. Why could you not come across the river to tell me that you were not dead?"

"Yes, you could have done that, Tom," said Mary.

"Would you, Tom?" said Aunt Polly. "If you had thought of it, would you have come to tell me?"

"Tom is always in a hurry," Mary said. "He never thinks."

■loving 形 愛情あふれる　■in a hurry 慌てて

# 18. トムのふしぎな夢

　トムの大計画はこうだった——他のふたりと一緒に家に戻り、それから教会へ行って、みんなが自分たちのために祈るのを聞くのだ。3人は夜のうちに川をわたって、朝まで森に隠れていた。それから教会へ行って、みんなが来るまで眠っていた。そして、いちばん大事なときに姿をあらわしたのだ。

　次の日の朝、ポリーおばさんとメアリーは、トムにとてもやさしかった。食べたいものはなんでも食べさせてもらえた。みんなはたくさん話した。ポリーおばさんが言った。
　「いまだから笑えるけどね、トム。でもこんなに心配させるなんて、あんまりだよ。あんたは川をわたってきて、教会にいるあたしたちを驚かしただろ。だったらなんで、自分たちは死んでないって知らせに、川をわたってこれなかったの？」
　「そうね、やろうと思えばできたわよね、トム」とメアリー。
　「そうなの、トム？」とポリーおばさん。「もしそう思いついてたら、知らせに来てくれたかい？」
　「トムはいつだって、あわてんぼだから」とメアリーが言った。「そんなこと考えないのよ」

## 18. Tom's Wonderful Dream

"Sid would have thought. And Sid would have come. Tom, one day you will be sorry. You will wish that you had cared more for me. But then it will be too late."

"I do care for you," said Tom. "I wish that I had thought. But I dreamed about you."

"A cat does that. What did you dream?"

"I dreamed that I saw you sitting there by the bed. Sid and Mary were sitting with you. And I dreamed that Joe Harper's mother was here."

"She was, one night. Did you dream any more?"

"Yes. But I can't remember all of it."

"Try, Tom. Try to remember."

"You said that the door must be open because you could feel the wind coming in. You said that was strange. And you told Sid—"

"What did I tell Sid, Tom?"

"You told him—oh, you told him to close the door. And you were talking about me. I remember better now. You said that I was not bad. You said that I was only wild and full of life like a—like any young animal."

"I am surprised! And some people say that dreams are never true. Tell me more, Tom."

"And then you began to cry."

"Yes, I did. I did."

■care for 〜のことを心配する　■any more もっと、それ以上

## 18. トムのふしぎな夢

「シッドなら考えただろうにねえ。それにシッドなら言いに来ただろうよ。トム、いつかおまえは後悔するよ。あたしのことをもっと心配してやればよかったと、思うにちがいないよ。でも、そのときにはもう遅いんだよ」

「ぼく、おばさんのこと心配してるよ」とトム。「もっと考えればよかったと思うけど。でも、おばさんの夢を見たよ」

「夢くらい、ネコだって見るよ。どんな夢を見たの？」

「おばさんがベッドのそばにすわってる夢だよ。シッドとメアリーもすわってた。それから、ジョー・ハーパーのお母さんもここにいたよ」

「おや、たしかにいたよ、あの晩にね。他にも何か見たかい？」

「うん。でも全部は思い出せないよ」

「やってごらん、トム。ほら、思い出してごらんよ」

「風が入ってくるから、きっとドアが開いてるんだって、おばさんが言ってた。おかしいねえ、って。それで、シッドに言ったんだ——」

「シッドになんて言ったって、トム？」

「シッドにね——そうだ、ドアを閉めるように言ったんだ。それから、ぼくの話をしてた。だんだん思い出してきたよ。おばさんがぼくのことを、そんなに悪い子じゃないって言ったんだ。ただわんぱくで、元気がよすぎるだけだって、まるで——動物の子みたいにね」

「まあ、驚いた！　夢なんか信じられないっていう人もいるのにね。もっと話しておくれ、トム」

「それから、おばさんは泣きだしたんだ」

「そうだよ、泣いたよ、泣いたよ」

## 18. Tom's Wonderful Dream

"Then Mrs. Harper began to cry. She said that Joe was good also. And then you told about me giving the Painkiller to the cat. And then everyone talked about finding our bodies, and praying in church on Sunday."

"It is all true!"

"And Mrs. Harper went home. And you prayed for me—and I could see you and hear every word. You went to bed, and I was very sorry for you. And I had a letter for you. It was on a piece of wood. On the wood were the words, 'We are not dead—we are away being pirates.' I gave you a kiss and went away again."

"Did you, Tom? Did you?" She gave him a big hug.

"It was very kind, but it was only a dream," said Sid.

"Be quiet, Sid! And Tom, here is a big apple for you. And now, children, go to school."

Tom walked slowly, feeling that everyone was watching him. Smaller boys followed him, happy to be seen with him. Boys his own age wished they had sun-tanned skin and were famous like him.

Tom decided that he was no longer interested in Becky Thatcher. He was happy being famous. When Becky arrived at school, Tom pretended not to see her. But he saw her playing with other boys and girls. And she often came near to him and looked at him.

■give someone a big hug （人を）ぎゅっと抱きしめる　■sun-tanned 形 日焼けした
■pretend 動 〜のふりをする

## 18. トムのふしぎな夢

「そしたら、ハーパーさんが泣きだしたんだ。ジョーもいい子だって言ってね。そんでもって、おばさんが、ぼくがネコに『痛みどめ』を食べさせた話をした。それからみんなで、ぼくたちの体をさがす話や、日曜日に教会で祈る話なんかをしてたんだ」

「まあ、全部そのとおりだよ!」

「そのあとハーパーさんが家に帰った。そして、おばさんはぼくのために祈ってくれたんだ——目の前に見えたし、お祈りだって全部聞こえたよ。おばさんはベッドに入ったけど、とってもかわいそうだったなあ。ぼくは手紙を持ってたんだ。板切れに書いたやつ。板切れには、こう書いてあったんだ。『ぼくたちは死んでません——遠くで海賊になっています』って。ぼくはおばさんにキスをして、また出ていったんだ」

「そうだったの、トム? ほんとに?」おばさんはトムをぎゅっと抱きしめた。

「へえ、ずいぶんやさしいんだね、でも、ただの夢だろ」とシッドが言った。

「おだまり、シッド! さあ、トム、大きなリンゴをあげようね。さあさあ、子どもたち、もう学校に行きなさい」

トムは悠々と歩きながら、みんなに注目されているのを感じた。年下の子どもたちが後ろについてきて、トムと一緒にいるところを見せたがった。同い年の少年たちは、自分たちもトムのように日に焼けて、有名になれたらいいのにと思った。

トムは、もうベッキー・サッチャーなんか気にかけないぞ、と心に決めた。有名になれて、うれしかったのだ。ベッキーが学校についたとき、トムは気がつかないふりをした。でも、ベッキーが他の男の子や女の子と遊んでいるのを、ちらちらと見ていた。ベッキーもしょっちゅうトムのそばへやってきて、トムのほうに目をやった。

## 18. Tom's Wonderful Dream

And he began talking to Amy Lawrence.

Becky tried to go away from him, but her feet would not move. They carried her near to the group around Tom. She said to one of the girls, "Mary, where were you yesterday? I wanted to tell you about the picnic."

"Oh, who's picnic?"

"My mother is going to let me have one."

"I hope that she will let me come."

"I may ask anyone I want. I want you and all my friends to come." She looked at Tom, but he was talking to Amy Lawrence. Others in the group began asking if they could go. Soon everyone had asked. Only Tom and Amy had not asked. Tom turned away.

Becky was sad and wanted to cry. She went away alone to think what to do.

When Tom saw her again, she and a boy called Alfred Temple were sitting together looking at a book. Now Tom suddenly wanted to stop talking to Amy. He left her and went to look again at Becky and Alfred. Becky pretended not to see Tom. But she saw him, and she was happy.

"That Alfred Temple!" Tom thought. "And his fine clothes! I will catch him! And I will—"

■ask if one could 〜してもいいかと聞く　■turn away 背を向ける

## 18. トムのふしぎな夢

　すると、トムはエイミー・ローレンスに話しかけだすのだった。
　ベッキーはトムから離れて行こうとしたが、足が動こうとしなかった。みんなに押されるようにして、トムのまわりの子どもたちに近づいた。そしてその中の女の子に話しかけた。「ねえ、メアリー、昨日はどこにいたの？　ピクニックの話をしたかったのに」
「あら、だれのピクニック？」
「うちのお母さんが、あたしにピクニックさせてくれるって」
「いいなあ、あたしも行っていいかしら」
「あたしが呼びたい人はだれでも呼んでいいのよ。あなたにも、それから友だちみんなにも来てほしいわ」ベッキーはトムを見たが、トムはエイミー・ローレンスと話していた。まわりにいた他の子どもたちが、ピクニックに行ってもいいかと聞きだした。やがてみんながピクニックに招かれた。トムとエイミーだけが招かれないままだった。トムは背を向けて行ってしまった。
　ベッキーは悲しくて泣きたいほどだった。どうしたらいいか考えようと、みんなから離れて歩いていった。
　トムがまたベッキーを見かけたとき、ベッキーはアルフレッド・テンプルという男の子と一緒に、本を見ながらすわっていた。すると、トムはとたんにエイミーと話すのがいやになった。トムはエイミーをほったらかしにして、ベッキーとアルフレッドのようすをまた見に行った。ベッキーは、トムに気がつかないふりをした。だけどベッキーは気がついていた。そしてうれしかったのだ。
　「アルフレッド・テンプルめ！」とトムは思った。「おしゃればっかりしてさ！　そのうち、とっちめてやる！　そんでもって──」

## 18. Tom's Wonderful Dream

He began hitting the air as if he were fighting with the other boy.

At noon Tom went home. Becky again looked at the book with Alfred, hoping that Tom would see them. But Tom did not.

Suddenly she began to cry. She left Alfred and walked away.

Alfred followed, hoping to find some way to make her happy again. But she said:

"Go away! I never want to see you again!"

Alfred was quick to understand. Becky had been trying to make Tom unhappy. He felt angry and went into the school. He saw one of Tom's books and thought how he could hurt Tom. He opened the book to the page they were going to study that afternoon. He tore the page so it looked like Tom had done it.

Becky, looking in the window, saw him do it. She thought of telling Tom. Then she decided that she would not. She would let the teacher hit Tom for tearing his book.

■as if あたかも〜かのように　■way to 〜する方法　■tore 動tear（〜を引き裂く）の過去

## 18. トムのふしぎな夢

　トムは他の男の子と戦っているように、空中を殴りだした。

　お昼の時間になったのでトムは家に帰った。ベッキーはまたアルフレッドと本を見ていたが、トムがそれを見ていたらいいのに、と思っていた。でも、トムはこちらをふり向かなかった。
　そのとたん、ベッキーは泣きだした。そしてアルフレッドをおいたまま、歩いていってしまった。
　アルフレッドはあとを追いかけながら、どうにかしてベッキーの機嫌をなおせないかと思った。でもベッキーは言った。
「あっちへ行ってよ！ あんたなんか、もう会いたくないわ！」
　アルフレッドは、すぐにピンときた。ベッキーは、トムにやきもちを焼かせようとしていたのだ。アルフレッドは腹を立てて、学校の中へ入っていった。トムの本を見て、どうやって仕返ししてやろうかと考えた。本を開き、今日の午後に習うところをさがした。そしてそのページをやぶき、トムが自分でやったかのように見せかけた。

　ベッキーは窓からのぞいていたので、アルフレッドのしたことを見ていた。トムに言わなくちゃ、と思った。でも、やっぱり言わないことに決めた。トムなんて、本をやぶいたことで先生に叩かれたらいいんだわ。

# 19 Tom Tells the Truth

Tom arrived home feeling very sad. His aunt's first words made him feel more sad.

"Tom, I want to hit you!"

"Aunt Polly, what have I done?"

"I went to see Mrs. Harper to tell her about your dream. Joe had already told her that you were here that night. I believed your story was a dream. Why did you say it was a dream?"

"Aunt Polly, I wish I had not done it. I did not think."

"Oh, child, you never think. You never think of anything but yourself. "

"Aunt Polly, I know that it was bad. But I did not plan to be bad. And I did not come here that night to laugh at you. I came to tell you that we were not dead. I did not want you to be sad."

"Tom, I would like to believe that. But I don't think that you had such a thought."

■anything but《否定を伴って》〜の他は何も (ない)　■would like to 〜したい

# 19. トム、白状する

　トムはとても悲しい気分で家についた。そして、おばさんの最初のひとことを聞いて、さらに悲しくなった。
「トム！　ぶったたいてやりたいよ！」
「ポリーおばさん、ぼくが何したっていうの？」
「ハーパーさんとこへ行って、あんたの話をしたんだよ。そしたら、あんたがあの夜ここにいたって、ジョーがすっかり話してたんだ。あの話は夢だって、あたしは信じてたのに。どうして夢なんて言ったの？」
「ポリーおばさん、あんなことしなけりゃよかったと思ってるよ。ぼくって、考えなしだね」
「ああ、あんたって子は、いつだって考えなしだよ。自分のことしか考えないんだからね」
「ポリーおばさん、悪いことしたってわかってるよ。でも、わざとじゃないんだ。あの夜ここへ来たのも、おばさんのことを笑うためなんかじゃないよ。ぼくたち死んでないって、知らせるために来たんだ。おばさんを悲しませたくなかったんだよ」
「トム、あたしはそのことばを信じたいよ。でもね、あんたがそんなこと考えるとは思えないんだよ」

## 19. Tom Tells the Truth

"Yes, I did, I did. It is true. I wanted to save you from being sad."

"Then why did you not tell me, child?"

"You began talking of Sunday and all the people praying for us in the church. And I began thinking about going there on Sunday. And I put my letter in my pocket and went away."

"What letter?"

"The letter to tell you that we were pirates. I wish now that you had opened your eyes when I gave you a kiss."

"Did you kiss me, Tom? Are you sure?"

"Yes, I did, Aunt."

"Why?"

"Because I loved you and you were crying in your sleep and I was sorry."

The words sounded true. The old lady said, "Kiss me again, Tom! And then go to school."

When he was gone, she looked at his little coat. In the pocket she found a piece of wood with writing on it. She read the words and tears fell from her eyes. Then she said, "Now I can forget anything bad that boy does. I could forget a million bad things."

■now that 今や〜だから　■sound 動 〜に聞こえる、〜に思われる

## 19. トム、白状する

「考えたよ、考えたって。ほんとだよ。おばさんが悲しまないようにしたかったんだ」

「じゃあ、どうして知らせてくれなかったの、坊や？」

「日曜日に教会で、みんながぼくたちのために祈ってくれるっていう話を始めただろ。だったら日曜日にあそこへ行ってやろうって、思うようになったんだ。それで手紙をポケットに入れて、出ていったんだよ」

「なんの手紙？」

「ぼくたちが海賊になったって知らせる手紙だよ。あーあ、ぼくがおばさんにキスしたとき、目を覚ましてくれてたらよかったのになあ」

「あたしにキスをしたのかい、トム？ ほんとうに？」

「うん、ほんとだよ、おばさん」

「どうして？」

「だって、おばさんのことが大好きだし、おばさんが泣きながら眠ってるから、すまないなって思ったんだ」

このことばは、ほんとうらしかった。おばさんは言った。「もういちどキスしておくれ、トム！ それから、学校に行っておいで」

トムが行ったあと、おばさんはトムの小さな上着を見た。ポケットの中に、何かを書いた板切れが入っていた。それを読むと、おばさんの目から涙がこぼれた。そしてこう言った。「ああこれで、あの子がしたどんな悪いことでも忘れられる。百万回の悪さだって、許してあげられるよ」

# 20 Becky Has a Problem

Tom was happy again. He started walking to school, and saw Becky Thatcher, also going to school. He ran to her and said:

"I am sorry I was bad this morning, Becky. I won't ever be like that again. Please let us be friends."

The girl stopped and looked into his face. "Go away, Mr. Thomas Sawyer. I will never speak to you again."

Then she started walking again. Tom was so surprised he could not think of anything to say. He was angry. If she were a boy, he would fight her.

Becky was also angry. Soon the teacher would hit Tom for tearing his book.

She did not know that she would soon have trouble too!

The teacher had a book that he was studying. Every day he would read some pages when he was not busy. Every boy and girl in the school knew about this book, but no-one had ever seen it. Now, as Becky passed the teacher's table, she saw the book. She opened it and began to look at it.

■not ever 決して〜ない　■let us be friends 友だちになろうよ

## 20. ベッキー、困ったことになる

　トムはまたうれしくなった。学校へ向かって歩きだすと、ベッキー・サッチャーも学校へ向かっているのが見えた。トムはベッキーに走り寄って、言った。
「今朝は、いじわるしてごめんよ、ベッキー。もうぜったい、あんなふうにしないからね。仲直りしてよ」
　女の子は立ち止まり、トムの顔をにらんだ。「あっち行ってよ、トマス・ソーヤーさん。あなたとは話したくないわ」
　そしてベッキーはまた歩きだした。トムはあんまりびっくりしたので、何を言えばいいか思いつかなかった。腹が立ってきた。ベッキーがもし男の子だったら、ケンカするところだ。
　ベッキーも怒っていた。もうすぐ先生が、本をやぶいたことでトムを叩くんだわ、いい気味。
　かわいそうにベッキーは、自分ももうすぐ困ったことになるとは、まるで知らなかったのだ！
　先生は自分の勉強のために本を持っていた。毎日、暇を見つけては数ページ読むのが習慣だった。どの子もみんな、この本のことを知っていたが、だれも開いて見たことがなかった。ところがこのとき、ベッキーが先生の机のそばを通ると、その本があったのだ。ベッキーは本を開いて中を見だした。

## 20. Becky Has a Problem

Suddenly Tom opened the door. Becky quickly closed the book. But her hand caught the page, and suddenly, it was in two pieces. Becky began to cry.

"You are bad, Tom Sawyer, to come and watch me! And now you will tell the teacher, and he will hit me. What should I do? I have never been hit in school. But I know what is going to happen to you. You wait and see!" Then she ran outside crying.

Tom said to himself: "How silly that girl is! Being hit in school is nothing. And I will not tell who opened the book. The teacher will ask who did it. He will call each name. And when he says the right one, he won't need an answer. He will see the answer in her face."

School began, and soon Tom's book was discovered. He said that he had not torn the page, but the teacher did not believe him. The teacher hit Tom, and Becky watched, trying to feel happy about this. But she almost stood up to say it was Alfred Temple.

One hour later, the boys and girls were busy with their books. The teacher opened his book. Tom looked at Becky. He wished that he could help her, but what could he do?

■You wait and see! 今に見ていろ。覚えておけ。　■say to oneself ひとりごとを言う

## 20. ベッキー、困ったことになる

 するといきなり、トムがドアを開いた。ベッキーはあわてて本を閉じた。でも本のページに手が引っかかって、そのとたん、ビリリッとふたつに裂けてしまったのだ。ベッキーは泣きだした。
「あなたが悪いのよ、トム・ソーヤー、あなたが入ってきて見たりするからよ！ 先生に言いつけるんでしょ、そしたら、あたし先生に叩かれるわ。どうしよう？ 学校で叩かれたことなんかないのに。だけど、あなたがどんな目にあうか、あたし知ってるのよ。いまにわかるわ！」そしてベッキーは泣きながら外へ走っていった。
 トムはぶつぶつ、つぶやいた。「バカなやつだなあ！ 学校でぶたれるくらい、なんでもないじゃないか。それに、だれが本を開けたか言いつけたりするもんか。だれがやったか先生のほうが聞くさ。ひとりひとりの名前を呼んでさ。そんでもって、犯人の名前を呼んだら、返事なんかいらないんだ。顔を見たらわかっちゃうんだから」
 午後の授業が始まると、すぐにトムの本がやぶれているのが見つかった。トムはやぶいていないと言ったが、先生は信じてくれなかった。先生がトムをムチで叩いた。ベッキーはそれを見て、いい気味だと思おうとした。でも、とてもそうは思えなくて、もう少しで立ち上がって、アルフレッド・テンプルがやったんです、と言いそうだった。
 1時間後、子どもたちはみんな教科書の問題にかかりっきりになっていた。先生が自分の本を開いた。トムはベッキーのほうを見た。助けてやりたいけど、いったいどうしたらいいんだろう？

## 20. Becky Has a Problem

The teacher stood before the school. Everyone was afraid of him.

"Who did this to my book?"

No one spoke.

"Benjamin Rogers?"

"No."

"Joe Harper?"

"No."

"Amy Lawrence?"

"No."

"Gracie Miller?"

"No."

The next name was Becky Thatcher. Tom was afraid, but he saw that she was more afraid.

"Becky Thatcher, look at me! Did you do this to my book?"

Tom jumped to his feet and shouted, "I did it." Everyone looked at him. They could not believe what they had heard.

Tom stood up to be hit. But the look of surprise, thanks and love in Becky's eyes was enough for being hit a hundred times.

■afraid of 〜を怖がる　■jump to one's feet 飛び上がるように立ち上がる

## 20. ベッキー、困ったことになる

　先生が生徒たちのまえに、すっくと立ち上がった。みんなは震えあがった。

「わたしの本をやぶったのは、だれかね？」
だれも答えない。
「ベンジャミン・ロジャーズ？」
「いいえ」
「ジョー・ハーパー？」
「いいえ」
「エイミー・ローレンス？」
「いいえ」
「グレイシー・ミラー？」
「いいえ」
　次の名前はベッキー・サッチャーだ。トムはこわかったけれど、ベッキーがもっとこわがっているのがわかった。
「ベッキー・サッチャー、こっちを見なさい！　きみが本をやぶったのかね？」

　トムが飛びあがるように立ち上がって叫んだ。「ぼくがやりました」　みんながトムを見つめた。いま聞いたことが信じられなかった。
　トムは席を立って、ムチで叩かれた。でもベッキーの目に、驚きと感謝と愛しい思いが浮かんでいるのを見ると、100回叩かれても平気だと思った。

# 21

## Old Muff's Friends

It was the school summer holidays.

The days were too long. Tom did not have enough to do.

He decided to write a diary of everything that happened. But nothing happened for three days. He decided that a diary was no good.

Becky Thatcher was living in another town with her father and her mother during the summer.

Tom still remembered the killing in the graveyard. It made him sick.

For two weeks Tom stayed in bed. He was very ill. He was interested in nothing. Then he was better. But after a day he was ill again. He was in bed for three more weeks.

In the warm, quiet village something began to happen. A judge was coming to listen to the story of the killing in the graveyard. He would decide what to do about Muff Potter.

Every person in the village talked of this. And Tom felt afraid. He took Huck to a quiet place. He wanted to be sure that Huck had not told the story.

■graveyard 名墓地　■judge 名判事

# 21. マフじいさんの友だち

　夏休みがやってきた。
　夏の日々は長すぎるくらいだ。トムはすることがなくなって退屈だった。
そこで起こったことを全部日記に書くことにした。ところが、3日間という
もの、何も起こらなかった。日記なんてダメだ、とトムは決めつけた。

　ベッキー・サッチャーは夏のあいだ、両親と一緒に他の町ですごしていた。

　トムは、墓地での殺人事件をまだ覚えていた。そのことを考えると、気分
が悪くなった。
　2週間のあいだ、トムはベッドで寝ていた。重い病気になってしまったのだ。
何もする気になれない。そのあとよくなったけれど、1日たつと、また具合が
悪くなった。さらに3週間も寝ていなければならなかった。
　蒸し暑い静かな村では、何かが起ころうとしていた。墓地での殺人事件の
聞き取りのために、判事がやってくるのだ。そしてマフ・ポッターの処分を
決めることになっていた。
　村じゅうが、この話でもちきりだった。トムはこわくてたまらなかった。ト
ムはハックを静かな場所へつれだした。ハックがあのことをだれにも話して
ないか、確かめたかったのだ。

## 21. Old Muff's Friends

"Huck, have you told about—that?"

"Oh. No, I have not."

"Never a word?"

"Never a word. Why do you ask?"

"I was afraid."

"Tom Sawyer, we would not live two days if that story was told. You know that."

"Huck, could any person make you tell?"

"If I wanted Indian Joe to kill me, they could make me tell."

"Good! I think that we are safe if we do not talk."

"What talk have you heard, Huck?"

"Talk? It is all Muff Potter, Muff Potter, Muff Potter."

"I hear the same talk. They are going to hang him. Do you feel sorry for him sometimes?"

"Almost always—almost always. He has never done anything to hurt another person. He only fishes to get some money so that he can get drunk. He is really good. Once he gave me a fish, when he really did not have enough for himself. And he helped me at other times when I needed help."

"He helped me, also, Huck. He helped me to catch fish. I wish that I could get him out of jail."

■never a ~ 一つの〜も（ない）　■hang 動 〜を絞首刑にする　■so that 〜できるように　■get drunk 酔っ払う　■jail 名 牢屋、拘置所

## 21. マフじいさんの友だち

「ハック、だれかにしゃべったか——あのことをさ？」
「まさか。おいら、しゃべってないよ」
「ひとことも？」
「ひとこともさ。なんで聞くんだ？」
「こわかったんだよ」
「トム・ソーヤー、もししゃべったら、おいらたち2日だって生きてられないぜ。わかってるだろ」
「ハック、ひょっとしてだれかが、おまえにしゃべらせることができるか？」
「もし、おいらがインジャン・ジョーに殺されたいなら、しゃべらせることができるだろうな」
「よし！ おれたちさえだまってたら、きっと安全だと思うよ」
「ところで、どんな話を聞いた、ハック？」と、さらにトムは言った。
「うわさ話か？ どこへ行っても、マフ・ポッター、マフ・ポッター、マフ・ポッターばっかりさ」
「おれも同じうわさを聞いたよ。ポッターじいさんを、しばり首にするつもりなんだ。ときどき、じいさんに悪いなって思わないか？」
「ほとんど、いつもだよ——ほとんど、いつも思ってる。ポッターじいさんは、だれかに悪さしたことなんかないんだ。釣った魚を金にかえて、それで酒を飲んでるだけさ。ほんとに、いい人なんだ。まえだって、おいらに魚をくれたんだ。自分の分も十分ないのにさ。それに、他のときにも、おいらが困ってたら助けてくれたんだ」
「おれのことも助けてくれたよ、ハック。魚をつかまえるのを手伝ってくれたんだ。牢屋から出してあげられたらいいのになあ」

## 21. Old Muff's Friends

"We can't get him out, Tom. And if we did, they would catch him again."

"Yes...but he did not do it."

The boys talked for a long time, but it did not make them happy. As night came, they went to the jail. They went to the window and gave Potter some cigarettes. They had done this before.

He was always very happy to get their presents, and his thanks always hurt them. It hurt them even more when Potter said:

"You have been good to me, boys. Better than the others in this town. And I won't forget, I won't. Often I say to myself, 'I was good to all the boys. I showed them where the good fishing was. I was their friend when I could be a friend. And now they forget old Muff when he has trouble. But Tom does not forget, and Huck does not—they do not forget him,' I say, 'and I won't forget them.'

"But, boys, I did a bad thing. I was drunk. Now I must die for it. But we won't talk about that. I won't make you feel sad. You have been my friends.

"But I want to say this. Never get drunk. Then you won't ever be where I am now.

■even more ましてやなおさら〜である

## 21. マフじいさんの友だち

「おいらたちじゃ無理だよ、トム。それに、もしやっても、すぐにまたつかまるよ」

「そうだな……でも、ポッターじいさんは人殺しなんかやってないのに」

少年たちは長い間話しあっていたが、いくら話しても心が沈むばかりだった。夜になると、ふたりは牢屋へ向かった。窓のところへ行って、ポッターにタバコを渡した。まえにも、そうしたことがあったのだ。

ポッターはふたりのプレゼントを受け取ると、いつもとても喜んだ。ポッターがありがとうと言うと、ふたりの胸はいつも痛んだ。ポッターがこんなふうに言うと、もっとつらかった。

「おまえたちはいつも、やさしくしてくれるなあ、坊やたちよ。町の他の子どもらより、ずっとやさしいよ。おれ、忘れねえからな、ぜったい忘れねえ。おれ、よくひとりごとを言うのさ。『おれはどの子にもやさしくしてやった。いい釣り場だって教えてやった。友だちでいれるときは、子どもらの友だちだったのさ。でもこうして困ったことになると、あいつらはマフじいさんのことなんか忘れちまうんだ。でも、トムは忘れねえ、それからハックも忘れねえ——ふたりはマフじいさんのことを忘れねえ』ってな。『だから、おれもふたりのことを忘れねえぞ』」

「でもなあ、坊やたち、おれは悪いことをしたんだよ。酔っぱらっててさ。だから死ななきゃなんねえ。でも、その話はやめような。おまえたちを悲しませたくねえからさ。おまえたちはおれの友だちだからな」

「でも、これだけは言っとくよ。酔っぱらうんじゃねえぞ。そうすりゃ、いまおれがいるようなとこへ、入ったりしねえからな」

## 21. Old Muff's Friends

"You are the only ones who come here. Let me touch your hands. Little hands, and weak, but they have helped Muff Potter. And they would help him more if they could."

Tom went home feeling very, very sad. During the next two days he went to the town meeting house. The judge was listening to the story of the killing. Tom wanted to go inside, but stayed outside.

Huck was having the same experience.

They were careful not to meet each other. Tom listened when people came out. The news was always bad. At the end of the second day people said that Indian Joe's story never changed. Everyone knew what the judge would decide.

All the people in the village went to the meeting house the next morning. This was to be the important day. There was no hope for Potter. The judge arrived. And Indian Joe was there, too.

A man was asked about the killing. He said he saw Muff Potter washing his hands in the river. It was the morning after the killing.

Another man was asked to tell his story. He told about finding the knife near the doctor's body.

Another man spoke about the knife. He knew that it was Potter's knife.

■town meeting house 公会堂、町民集会所

## 21. マフじいさんの友だち

「ここへ来てくれるのは、おまえたちだけだよ。その手にさわらしてくれないか。小さな手だなあ、弱々しくてさ、でもマフ・ポッターを助けてくれた手だ。できたら、もっと助けてくれるといいんだけどな」

トムはたまらないほど悲しくなって、家に帰った。次の2日間、トムは町の公会堂へ行った。そこでは判事が殺人事件の聞き取りをしているのだ。トムは中に入りたかったが、外に立ってうろうろしていた。

ハックも同じような調子だった。

ふたりはお互い出会わないように気をつけていた。人々が出てくると、トムは聞き耳を立てた。話はいつもよくないものだった。2日目の終わりには、インジャン・ジョーの証言はもう覆せないと、みんな言っていた。判事がどんな判決を出すか、だれの目にも明らかだった。

翌朝、村じゅうの人々が公会堂へ向かった。重要な日になるはずだ。ポッターに望みはなかった。判事が到着した。そしてインジャン・ジョーもやってきた。

ある人が殺人事件について質問された。その人は、マフ・ポッターが川で手を洗っているのを見たと証言した。それは、殺人があった翌日の朝だった。

もうひとりの人が、証言を求められた。その人は、医者の死体のそばでナイフを見つけたことを話した。

別の人が、ナイフについて証言した。それがポッターのナイフであることを知っていたのだ。

## 21. Old Muff's Friends

A man who had studied law sat next to Muff Potter. He was there to help Potter. But he asked no questions as these men told their stories. It was strange.

More men told their stories. And the man next to Potter asked them no questions.

After a while, all the stories against Potter had been told. Then the man next to Potter stood up. He spoke to the judge:

"Sir, we planned to show that Muff Potter was drunk that night. We planned to show that he did not know what he was doing. But we have changed our plans. We wish to ask Thomas Sawyer some questions."

Everyone was surprised. Potter was very surprised. Every eye was watching Tom. He stood up and walked to the front of the meeting house. He was afraid.

The questions began.

"Thomas Sawyer, where were you on the night of the killing?"

Tom looked at Indian Joe, and he could not speak. But then he felt stronger and said:

"In the graveyard!"

"Louder, please. Do not be afraid. You were—"

"In the graveyard."

He looked at Indian Joe's face. He saw a cold smile. Then it was gone.

■law 名法律　■against 前〜に不利に　■sir 名《男性への丁寧な呼びかけのことば》

## 21. マフじいさんの友だち

　法律にくわしい男の人が、マフ・ポッターの横にすわっていた。ポッターを助けるためにいるのだ。でも証人たちが証言しているのに、彼は何も質問しなかった。なんとも奇妙なことだった。
　さらに他の人たちの証言が続いた。ポッターの横にすわっている人は、やはり質問しなかった。
　しばらくすると、ポッターにとって不利な証言が出そろった。すると、ポッターの横の人が立ち上がった。彼は判事に言った。
　「判事どの、わたくしどもは、その夜マフ・ポッターが酔っていたことを示すつもりでした。そして、自分で何をしているのかわからない状態であったことを示そうと思っておりました。しかし、方針を変更いたしました。トマス・ソーヤーに質問したいと思います」
　だれもがびっくりした。ポッターもとても驚いた。全員の目がトムを見つめていた。トムは立ち上がり、公会堂のまえのほうへ歩いていった。こわくて、びくびくしていた。
　質問が始まった。
　「トマス・ソーヤー、殺人のあった夜、あなたはどこにいましたか？」
　トムはインジャン・ジョーのほうを見ると、何も言えなくなった。でもそのあと、勇気をふるいおこして言った。
　「墓地です！」
　「もっと大きな声で言ってください。こわがらなくていいですよ。あなたは——」
　「墓地にいました」
　トムはインジャン・ジョーの顔を見た。インジャン・ジョーは冷ややかに笑っていたが、しだいにその笑みが消えていった。

## 21. Old Muff's Friends

"Were you near Hoss Williams's grave?"

"Yes."

"Louder, please. How near were you?"

"As near as I am to you."

"Could you be seen?"

"No. I was in the trees near the grave."

"Was another person with you?"

"Yes. I went there with—"

"That is enough. We will call him when we need him. Did you carry something there?"

Tom did not answer.

"Speak, my boy. What did you carry there?"

"Only a—a—dead cat."

Some people laughed.

"We plan to show the bones of that cat. Now, my boy, tell us everything that happened—tell it as you wish, but tell it all and do not be afraid."

Tom began slowly. Everyone looked at him. Interest in his story became greater and greater.

"—and as the doctor hit Muff Potter and Muff Potter fell, Indian Joe jumped with the knife and—"

Indian Joe jumped through a window, and was gone.

■grave 図墓 ■as ~ as …と同じくらい~ ■my boy 坊や、ぼく ■as you wish 望み通りに

「ホス・ウィリアムズの墓のそばにいたんですね?」
「はい」
「さあ、もっと大きな声で。どれくらい近くにいましたか?」
「ぼくと、あなたのあいだくらいです」
「人から見られたと思いますか?」
「いいえ。お墓のそばの木の後ろに隠れてたんです」
「あなたと一緒にだれかいましたか?」
「はい。ぼくと一緒にいたのは——」
「ああ、それはいいですよ。必要になったら、その人も呼びますから。そこに何か持っていきましたか?」

トムは答えなかった。

「さあ、ぼく、話しておくれ。何か持っていきましたか?」
「そ、その、死んだネコだけです」

何人かが笑った。

「そのネコの骨は、のちほど提出するつもりです。さあ、ぼく、何があったか全部話してくれませんか——話したいようにでいいから、でも全部話すんだよ、こわがらずにね」

トムはゆっくり話しだした。全員がトムに注目した。トムの話は、みんなの興味をどんどん引きつけていくものだった。

「——それでお医者さまがマフ・ポッターを殴ったから、マフ・ポッターが倒れて、そしたらインジャン・ジョーがナイフを持って飛びかかって、そんで——」

そのときインジャン・ジョーが窓から飛びだして、逃げ去った。

# 22 Happy Days and Bad Nights

Tom was famous again. The old people loved him and the young people wished they were like him. His name was in the village newspaper.

Everyone was kind to Muff Potter. Tom's days were happy, but at night he dreamed of Indian Joe.

Poor Huck felt the same. Huck had not been called in the meeting-house but he was afraid. Huck did not trust anyone, because Tom had broken their promise.

Every day, Muff Potter's thanks made Tom glad that he had told his story. Every night he wished that he had not opened his mouth.

Sometimes Tom was afraid that Indian Joe would never be caught. He felt he could never be safe until Indian Joe was dead.

Indian Joe had not been found.

The days passed and Tom did not feel so afraid.

■poor 形 かわいそうな、気の毒な　■trust 動 信用する　■break one's promise 約束をやぶる

## 22. うれしい昼と、こわい夜

　トムはまた有名になった。大人の人たちはトムをほめそやし、子どもたちはトムのようになりたいと思った。トムの名前は、村の新聞にも載った。

　だれもがマフ・ポッターにやさしくなった。トムは毎日、昼のあいだは幸せだった。でも夜になると、インジャン・ジョーの夢を見た。
　かわいそうなことにハックも、同じような状態だった。ハックは公会堂の裁判で呼ばれていなかったが、それでもこわかったのだ。ハックはもう、だれも信じられなかった。トムが約束をやぶったからだ。
　毎日トムは、マフ・ポッターに感謝されるたびに、証言してよかったと思った。でも毎晩、口を開かなければよかったのに、と思うのだった。

　ときどきトムは、インジャン・ジョーがつかまらなかったらどうしようと、不安になった。インジャン・ジョーが死ぬまでは、けっして安心できそうになかった。
　インジャン・ジョーはまだ見つかっていなかった。
　日々はすぎていき、やがてトムも、そんなにこわがらなくなっていった。

# 23 Dead People and Ghosts

There comes a time in every boy's life when he wants to hunt for gold that pirates have put deep in the earth.

Tom met Huck Finn who agreed to do anything that would take time but not money.

"Where can we find gold?" said Huck.

"Oh, only in very special places. Sometimes on islands, sometimes in old boxes under an old, dead tree, but usually under the floor in an old house."

"Who puts it there?"

"People who take it away from other people."

"Why do they put it in the ground? If I were rich, I would spend my money and enjoy it."

"I would too. But these people are different."

"Why don't they return and get it?"

"They think they will, but they forget where it is. Or they die."

■earth 图大地、陸地　■take time 時間がかかる

## 23. 死人と幽霊

　どんな少年でも、海賊が地中深くに隠した金貨を、この手で見つけたいと思うときがあるものだ。
　トムはハック・フィンに会った。ハックは、時間がかかっても金のかからないことなら、なんでも一緒にやってくれるのだ。
　「どこで金貨を見つけるんだ？」とハック。
　「そりゃあ、とっても特別なところだけさ。どっかの島だったり、古くて枯れた木の下に埋めた古い箱の中だったりさ。でもたいていは、古い家の床の下にあるんだ」
　「だれがそんなとこに金貨をおくんだよ？」
　「他の人から取ったやつらさ」
　「なんで土ん中に隠すんだ？ おいらなら、金がいっぱいあったら使って楽しむけどな」
　「おれもだよ。でも、こういうやつらは、ちがうんだ」
　「なんで取りに戻らないんだろ？」
　「もちろんそのつもりさ、でもどこにあるか忘れちゃうんだ。それか、死んじゃうのさ」

## 23. Dead People and Ghosts

"How are you going to find it, Tom? Where will you look?"

"We tried looking for gold on the island when we were pirates. I know where there is a very old house. And there are old, dead trees everywhere."

"How do you know which tree to choose?"

"Choose all of them!"

"Tom, we shall be working all summer!"

"What is wrong with that? We could find a hundred dollars. Or gold. How would you like that?"

Huck looked excited. "Give me the hundred dollars, and you can have the gold."

The boys got some gardening things. Then they walked to an old, dead tree outside the village. They were very hot and sat down to rest.

Tom said, "Huck, if we find some money, what will you do with it?"

"Spend it! Before my father takes it and spends it. What will you do with yours?"

"I will marry."

"Marry! Tom, you would be mad. Think of my father and mother. They were fighting all the time."

■What is wrong with 〜のどこがいけないのですか？　■gardening 名園芸　■mad 形気が狂って　■all the time いつも、四六時中

## 23. 死人と幽霊

「どうやって見つけるんだ、トム？ どこをさがすつもりさ？」

「おれたちが海賊だったときは、島で金貨をさがそうとしたよな。今度はさ、すごく古い家があるところを知ってるんだ。そんでもって、そこには古くて枯れた木がそこらじゅうにあるんだぜ」

「どの木を選んだらいいか、どうやってわかるんだよ？」

「どの木も全部だよ！」

「トム、それじゃあ、夏じゅう働かなきゃなんないぜ！」

「それがどうしたのさ？ 100ドル見つけるかもしれないんだぜ。それか金貨だ。さあ、どうする？」

ハックは興奮してきたようだった。「おいらには100ドルくれよ。金貨はおまえにやるから」

少年たちは庭仕事用のシャベルやつるはしを持ってきた。それから村のはずれの、古くて枯れた木のところへ歩いていった。掘っているうちに、とても暑くなってきたので、すわって休憩した。

トムが言った。「ハック、もし金が見つかったら、おまえどうする？」

「使うさ！ おやじが取って使っちまうまえにな。おまえはどうするんだ？」

「おれは結婚するんだ」

「結婚だって！ トム、頭がおかしくなったんじゃないか。おいらのオヤジとオフクロのことを考えてみろよ。いつだってケンカしてたんだぜ」

## 23. Dead People and Ghosts

"The girl I will marry won't fight."

"Tom, they are all the same. Who is she?"

"I won't tell you now."

"If you marry, I will be sadder than I am now."

"No, you won't. You will come to live with me. Now we must start working."

They worked for half an hour, but found no box of money. They worked for another half hour. Then Huck said:

"Is the money always so deep in the ground?"

"Not always. I don't think this is the right place."

They began again near another tree.

"Where shall we try next?" Huck said.

"There is an old tree on Cardiff Hill next to Mrs. Douglas's house."

"That might be a good place. But won't she take the money away from us? It is her land."

"If you find money in the ground, it's yours. It is not the land owners'."

They worked in the new place. After a while Tom said:

"We must be in the wrong place again. Maybe we should work at night."

■take away 取り上げる　■land owner 地主

## 23. 死人と幽霊

「おれが結婚する女の子は、ケンカなんかしないさ」
「トム、女の子なんてみんな同じだと思うけどな。その子はだれだ？」
「いまは言わないよ」
「おまえが結婚したら、おいら、いまより寂しくなるなあ」
「そんなことないさ。一緒に住めばいいんだ。さあ、仕事を始めなきゃ」

ふたりは半時間働いたが、金貨の箱は見つからなかった。もう半時間働いた。そのあとハックが言った。
「金貨ってのは、いつもこんなに土の中深くに埋まってんのか？」
「そうとも限らないさ。ここじゃないんだと思うな」
ふたりは、もうひとつの木のそばを、また掘りはじめた。
「次は、どこをやってみるんだ？」と、ハックが言った。
「カーディフ丘のダグラスさんの家の横に、古い木があるんだ」

「そりゃあ、いいかもしれないな。でも、ダグラスさんに金を取られないかな？ ダグラスさんの土地だしさ」
「土の中に埋まってる金を見つけたら、自分のものになるんだ。土地の持ち主のものじゃないのさ」
ふたりは新しい場所で掘りはじめた。しばらくしてトムが言った。
「きっと、おれたち、またまちがったんだな。夜にやったほうがいいかもな」

## 23. Dead People and Ghosts

The boys stopped work and returned to the tree that night. It was a very quiet place. They began to work.

They worked hard, but didn't find anything. Tom said: "Huck, we are wrong again."

"We should stop," Huck said. "I do not like the night. I am afraid."

"I feel the same, Huck. Can we try another place?"

"Where?"

"The old house."

"Tom, I am afraid of old houses. Let's go to the house during the day."

少年たちはいったん掘るのをやめて、夜に木のところへ戻ってきた。とても静かな場所だった。ふたりは仕事を始めた。
　ふたりは一生懸命働いたが、何も見つからなかった。トムが言った。「ハック、またまちがってるみたいだ」
「もうやめたほうがいいな」とハックが言った。「夜はきらいだ。おっかないよ」
「おれもだよ、ハック。もうひとつ、他の場所をやろうか？」
「どこだ？」
「あの古い、オンボロ屋敷だよ」
「トム、おいら、古い家はおっかないよ。昼間に行こうぜ」

# 24
## Sleeping Ghosts
## —A Box Full of Gold

On Saturday afternoon the boys went to the old house. It was very quiet and they were afraid.

Quietly they went in. They did not speak. They looked around with interest.

They put their tools by the door.

Then they wanted to look at the room above.

They found nothing up there and started to go down when they heard a sound.

"We must run!"

"We can't. They are coming in."

The boys were on the floor, looking down into the room through holes. They were afraid.

Two men entered. Both boys knew one of them. He was very old. He had long white hair, and a white beard. The village people thought it sad that he could not hear and could not speak.

■tool 名道具 ■beard 名あごひげ

## 24. 眠る幽霊と金貨の箱

　土曜日の午後、少年たちはオンボロ屋敷へ行った。とても静かだったので、ふたりはこわくなった。
　そっと家の中へ入っていく。ふたりはしゃべらなかった。しげしげと、あたりを見まわした。
　道具をドアのそばにおいた。
　ふたりは上の階の部屋が見たくなって、あがっていった。
　そこに何もないのがわかったので、下へおりようとすると、物音が聞こえた。
　「逃げなきゃ！」
　「無理だよ。中に入ってくる」
　少年たちは床に突っ伏して、床にあいた穴から下の部屋をのぞいた。こわくてたまらなかった。
　ふたりの男が入ってきた。そのうちのひとりは、トムもハックも知っていた。ずいぶん年を取った男だ。白髪が長くのびて、白いあごひげを生やしていた。耳も聞こえず口もきけないので、村人たちが、かわいそうに思っていた。

## 24. Sleeping Ghosts—A Box Full of Gold

The other man was a stranger. He was wearing very old clothes. His face was not kind. He was talking as they entered.

The two men sat, with their backs against the wall.

"No," said the stranger. "I do not like it. They will catch us."

"You are mad!" said the man who everyone thought could not hear or speak. "You are afraid!"

Now the boys were very afraid. This man was Indian Joe!

Joe said, "We were not caught before."

"But that was different."

"They may catch us here in this house," Joe said. "I wanted to leave here yesterday. But those boys were playing on Cardiff Hill. They would have seen us."

"Those boys" were Tom and Huck. They were even more afraid. What would have happened to them yesterday, if they had come to this house? They wished that they had waited a year before coming.

The two men had brought some food, and they began to eat.

■ with one's back against ～にもたれて

## 24. 眠る幽霊と金貨の箱

　もうひとりの男は知らない人だった。とても古ぼけた服を着ていた。こわい顔をしている。入ってくるとき、何かを話していた。
　ふたりの男は、壁にもたれてすわった。
　「いやだね」と見知らぬ男が言った。「そいつは気に入らねえ。つかまっちまうぜ」
　「バカ言うんじゃねえ！」聞くことも話すこともできないと、みんなが思っていた男が言った。「こわいんだな！」
　この声に、少年たちは身震いするほどぞっとした。この男は、インジャン・ジョーだ！
　ジョーは言った。「まえだって、つかまらなかったじゃねえか」
　「だけどさ、あれとはちがうぜ」
　「この家にいたって、つかまるかもしれねえんだ」とジョーは言った。「昨日のうちに、出ていきたかったんだがな。あのガキどもが、カーディフ丘で遊んでやがったんだ。おれたちを見たかもしれねえからな」
　「あのガキども」とは、トムとハックのことだ。ふたりは、もっとこわくなった。もし昨日この家に来ていたら、どんなことになっていただろう？　なんなら1年待ってから来てもよかったと、ふたりは思った。
　ふたりの男は食べ物を持ってきていたので、食べだした。

## 24. Sleeping Ghosts—A Box Full of Gold

After a while Joe said, "When it is dark, go home. Wait there until you hear from me. And we will do the job we planned. And then we will run. Far away. Now I need sleep. You stay here and make sure it is safe."

He went to sleep. Soon the other man was sleeping too.

"Now is our chance—let's go!" said Tom.

Huck said. "I can't. I am too afraid."

Tom started to leave alone. But the old floor made lots of sounds, so he stopped.

The boys could not leave.

Slowly it became night.

Indian Joe woke up. He said, "It is time for us to go. What shall we do with our money? Shall we leave it here? Six hundred dollars is heavy to carry."

His friend agreed and took out a big bag of money.

The boys became interested. Six hundred dollars would make the boys rich! And they knew where Indian Joe was putting it.

Indian Joe found the boys' tools and used them to make a hole in the ground. The boys watched quietly. Now they were very glad they were there!

■make sure 確認する、確かめる　■take out 取り出す

## 24. 眠る幽霊と金貨の箱

　しばらくして、ジョーが言った。「暗くなったら、家に帰れ。連絡するまでそこで待ってろ。それから、おれたちは計画どおり仕事にかかるんだ。そのあと逃げるのさ。遠くへな。さて、おれは眠っとかないといけねえ。おまえ、ここにいて、見張っててくれ」
　ジョーは眠りについた。そのうち、もうひとりの男も眠りこんだ。
　「いまがチャンスだ──行こう！」とトム。
　ハックは言った。「できないよ。もう、おっかなくってさ」
　トムはひとりで行きかけた。でも、古い床が大きな音を立てたので、立ち止まった。
　少年たちは出ていくことができなかった。
　ゆっくりと、夜がやってきた。
　インジャン・ジョーが目を覚まして、言った。「さあ、行く時間だ。金はどうする？　ここにおいていくか？　600ドルは、持ち運ぶにゃ重いな」

　ジョーの相棒は賛成して、大きな金袋を取り出した。
　少年たちは、たちまち興味をひかれた。600ドルあれば、少年たちは大金持ちになれる！　しかも、インジャン・ジョーがどこに隠すかわかるのだ。

　インジャン・ジョーは少年たちの道具を見つけ、それを使って地面に穴を掘った。少年たちは音も立てずに見つめていた。いまでは、ここにいてよかったと、心底喜んでいた！

## 24. Sleeping Ghosts—A Box Full of Gold

Then the tool hit something hard.

"Look!" Indian Joe said.

"What is it?" said his friend.

"It is an old box," Joe said. He opened it. "It's full of money!"

The men took the box out of the hole and looked at the money.

"There are thousands of dollars here," said Indian Joe.

"Now we don't need to do that job in the village," said the other.

Indian Joe said, "You do not understand. I am not doing that job only for money. Wrong was done to me, and I am going to get even. I need your help. Go home until I tell you to come."

"What shall we do with this money? Put it in the ground again?"

"Yes. (The boys were happy.) No! (The boys were sad.) Where did these tools come from? Who was here? Let's put the money at Number Two place, under the cross."

"It is dark. Let's go."

■get even 仕返しする、借りを返す　■cross 图十字架

そのとき、シャベルが何か硬いものにあたった。
 「見ろ！」とインジャン・ジョーが言った。
 「なんだ？」とジョーの相棒。
 「古い箱だ」とジョーが言った。そしてふたを開けた。「金貨でいっぱいだぜ！」
 男たちは穴から箱を取り出し、金貨を見つめた。

 「何千ドルもあるぜ」とインジャン・ジョー。
 「これで、村であの仕事をしなくてもすむな」と、もうひとりの男。

 インジャン・ジョーが言った。「わかってねえな。金のためだけにするんじゃねえんだ。ひでえ目にあわされたから、仕返ししてやるのさ。おまえの助けがいるんだよ。おれが呼ぶまで、家に帰って待ってろ」

 「この金はどうする？　また土に埋めるか？」

 「そうだな。（少年たちは喜んだ。）いや、だめだ！（少年たちはがっかりした。）この道具はどっから持ってきたんだ？　ここにだれが来たんだ？　金は『2号』の場所におこうぜ。十字架の下にな」
 「暗くなる。さあ、行こうぜ」

## 24. Sleeping Ghosts—A Box Full of Gold

"Who do you think came here?" Indian Joe said. "Do you think they are still here?"

The boys were afraid.

Indian Joe put his hand on his knife and started to go up the steps.

The boys could not move. They heard Joe coming.

Then they heard the steps breaking, and Indian Joe fell down.

"No one is here," his friend said. "They ran away when they saw us coming."

Soon the two men left the house with the box of gold and the bag of dollars.

Tom and Huck watched them.

Now they were safe. They left the house and went back to the town.

In town, they decided to look for Indian Joe and find the Number Two place.

Tom had a bad thought. "Indian Joe said wrong was done to him and he was going to get even. Was he talking about us, Huck?"

Suddenly Huck was afraid too.

■put one's hand on 〜に手を掛ける　■go up 〜を上る

## 24. 眠る幽霊と金貨の箱

「だれが来たんだと思う？」とインジャン・ジョーが言った。「まだここにいると思うか？」

少年たちは震えあがった。

インジャン・ジョーはナイフの上に手をそえ、階段を上りだした。

少年たちは動けなかった。ジョーがやってくるのが聞こえる。

すると階段がこわれる音がして、インジャン・ジョーは下に落ちた。

「だれもいやしねえよ」と相棒が言った。「おれたちが来るのを見て、逃げたのさ」

やがてふたりの男は金貨の箱と金袋を持って、家を出ていった。

トムとハックは、その後ろ姿をじっと見つめていた。

もう大丈夫だ。ふたりは家をあとにし、町へ戻った。

町につくと、ふたりはインジャン・ジョーをさがして、「2号」の場所を突きとめようと決心した。

でも、トムの心に不吉な考えが浮かんだ。「インジャン・ジョーが、ひどい目にあったから仕返しするって言ってたよな。それって、おれたちのことかな、ハック？」

たちまちハックも、こわくなってきた。

## 覚えておきたい英語表現

> I shall never, never see him again. （p.126, 7行目）
> もう二度と決してトムに会えないんだわ。

【解説】shallは「〜だろう」「〜するだろう」と、未来を表現する助動詞です。しかし未来を表現する方法でshallを使うのは、アメリカ英語では一般的でなく、イギリス英語で主に見られる使い方です。しかもややかたく古風な印象を与えます。未来や意思を表す表現としては、willが主に使われるようになっています。

最近の教科書でも、なかなかshallそのものを目にする機会が少なくなって来たように感じます。せいぜい"Shall we 〜?"などで見るくらいで、shallよりもその過去形should「〜すべき」のほうが存在感を感じさせる気がします（shallに失礼？）。

p.130、3行目にはポリーおばさんが "And some person shall be me." と言っている場面があります。このshallは話し手の意思「〜するぞ」を意味し、とても強固な意志を感じさせる表現です。こちらも現代からするとかたい印象を与える言葉づかいです。

『トム・ソーヤー』の書かれた時代背景をよく表す単語だと思い取り上げました。

> Huck stood alone, not knowing what to do. （p.128, 下から2行目）
> ハックはどうしてよいかわからず、ひとりぼっちで立っていた。

【解説】knowingはknowの現在分詞です。分詞は動詞の変化した形で、現在分詞（Ving）と過去分詞（Vpp）の2つがあります。分詞で始まる語句全体が、副詞の働きをするものを「分詞構文」といいます。表す意味としては「〜なので（理由）」「〜した時に（時）」「〜しながら（同時）」などが主な例ですが、これにあてはめにくい文例も多数あるので、コンマの前後で2つ別々の文に分けて、意味がつながるように訳すとよいでしょう。

【例文】

Being tired, I stayed at home all day.
疲れていたので、一日中家にいたよ。

Seeing Mary, I was reminded of my daughter.
メアリーを見た時に［見たので］、私は娘のことを思い出した。

Thinking about the deadline, I'd better help you.
締め切りのことを考えたら、僕は君の手伝いをするべきだろうね。

この文はもともと"Huck stood alone because he didn't know what to do."でしょう。becauseの前後で主語が同じですから一方を省き、接続詞も省いて簡単な文にしてあります。否定の分詞構文は分詞の前にnotを残しておきます。
　分詞構文は難しく感じますが、"省きましたよ"という合図のために、動詞を分詞に変化させてあると考えればよいでしょう。「分詞構文」に苦手な印象をお持ちの方は「省けるところを省いて、シンプルな文にしましたよ」という合図だと思ってみてください。


> Becky had been trying to make Tom unhappy. （p.140, 11行目）
> ベッキーはトムに何とかやきもちをやかせようとしていた。

【解説】had + Vppで過去完了形です。これにbe + Ving「進行形」を加えてhad been Vingとしたものを「過去完了進行形」といいます。「（その時点まで）〜し続けていた」と訳します。
　try to 〜で「〜しようとする」という意味です。Scene 1で解説（p.68）したstop to Vとstop Vingを思い出して欲しいのですが、to Vは「未来志向」です。だからtry to Vは「Vしようとする」という意味になります。一方try Vingは「過去志向」ですから「試しにVしてみた」という意味です。
　日本語のニュアンスからも感じ取れますが、「Vしようとした」と言えば"結局Vできなかった"という意味合いを含むことがあります。一方try Vingは「試しにやってみた」わけですから"実際おこなった"場合に使います。
　ここでもto VとVingの持つ意味の違いを感じていただきたいと思います。


> I could forget a million bad things. （p.144, 下から2行目）
> 百万回の悪さだって忘れてあげられるよ。

【解説】Scene 2で解説（p.122）した仮定法過去形です。この言葉の前の台詞が"Now I can forget anything bad that boy does."です。こちらは"I can"と現在形であることに対して、次の台詞は"I could"と過去形になっています。仮定法らしさがよく表れた表現です。
　仮定法がなぜ現在のことは過去形、過去のことは過去完了（大過去）で表すかご存じ

## 覚えておきたい英語表現

ですか？　過去は現在の時点（地点）からすれば「遠い」ですよね。二度と帰れませんし。では仮定の話はどうでしょう？　例えば「自分が鳥である世界」なんて、現在の時点（地点）からは遠い世界の話ですね。「現在の時点（地点）」から遠いから「仮定法では現在のことも過去形」で表すのです。この「仮定の世界は遠い」感覚がポイントです。過去形、過去完了形とともに仮定法のイメージを私が授業で生徒に解説する際は、黒板に以下のような図を書きます。よろしければ参考にしてみて下さい。

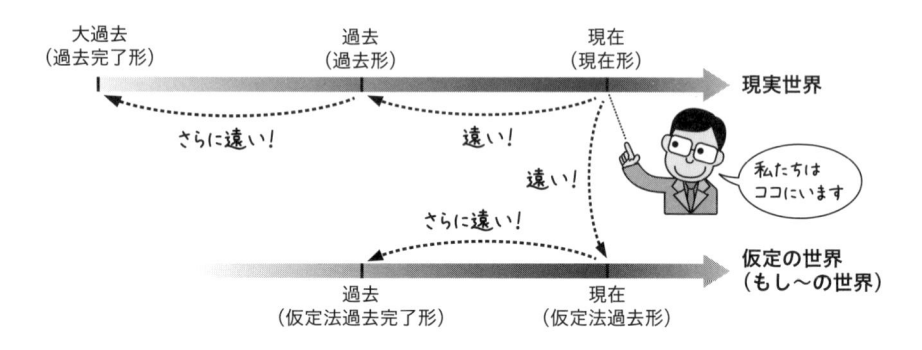

```
大過去              過去              現在
(過去完了形)       (過去形)          (現在形)
  ←‥‥‥‥‥‥‥‥‥‥‥‥‥‥‥‥‥‥‥‥‥‥‥→ 現実世界
      さらに遠い！      遠い！      ↓
                              遠い！    私たちは
                                        ココにいます
              さらに遠い！        ↓
  ←‥‥‥‥‥‥‥‥‥‥‥‥‥‥‥‥‥‥‥‥‥‥‥→ 仮定の世界
              過去              現在           （もし～の世界）
         (仮定法過去完了形)  (仮定法過去形)
```

　表題のポリーおばさんのセリフは、現実から遠いのでcanではなくcouldが使われているのです。さすがの（？）トムでも百万回も悪さはしていません。百万回なんて極端な数字は現実からは遠いので、canではなく仮定法で過去形にしたcouldを用いているのです。

　この小さな一語が「たとえありえないほどの悪さをたくさんしたとしても忘れられる」というポリーおばさんの気持ちをよく表しています。人情深いポリーおばさんに読者もほろっとさせられる名シーンです。

　仮定法は口語でも文語でも多用される重要な文法です。マスターすれば英語の楽しさが一層深まります。ぜひ頑張ってください。

# Scene 4

# 25 Bad Thoughts

Tom had bad dreams that night. Four times he had the gold in his hands. Four times he opened his eyes and had nothing. When he woke up everything was like a dream. The money was like a dream. He had never seen half a hundred dollars before. The day was like a dream. He decided to talk to Huck, but not to talk about the money. If it was a dream, Huck would not talk about it.

He found Huck fishing by the river. He looked very sad.

"Hello, Huck!"

"Hello, Tom."

No one said anything.

"Tom, if we had not put our tools by the door, we would have that money."

"It was not a dream, it was not a dream! But I almost wish that it was a dream."

"Dream! If Indian Joe had found us, you would know that it was not a dream!"

■thought 名 考え

## 25. 不吉な考え

　トムはその夜、いやな夢を見た。4回、トムは金貨を手に入れた。ところが4回とも、目を開けると何も持っていないのだ。目を覚ますと、何もかもが夢だったような気がした。金も夢だったように思えた。トムは、50ドルだって見たことがないのだ。その日じたい、夢だったような気がする。トムはハックと話すことに決めた。でも、金の話はしないでおこう。もし夢だったら、ハックはその話をしないだろう。

　トムは、ハックが川で釣りをしているのを見つけた。とても悲しそうだった。

「やあ、ハック！」

「やあ、トム」

　しばらくのあいだ、ふたりともだまっていた。

「トム、もしドアのそばに道具をおいてなかったら、あの金を取れたのになあ」

「夢じゃなかった、夢じゃなかったんだ！　でも、夢だったらよかったかもしれないなあ」

「夢だって！　もしインジャン・ジョーに見つかってたら、夢じゃないって、よくわかっただろうぜ！」

## 25. Bad Thoughts

"We must find him! Find the money! We must find his Number Two place. It could be the number of a house."

"No, Tom. The houses in this town do not have numbers."

"It could be the number of a hotel room."

"Yes! There are only two hotels here."

"You stay here, Huck. I will go and find Number Two."

Tom went into town. A young man was staying in room Number Two at the first hotel.

Room Number Two was closed at the second hotel. But a light had been seen in the window the night before.

"That room is Indian Joe's Number Two, Huck."

"I think you are right, Tom. What shall we do?"

Tom thought.

"We must wait and try to go in at night. If you see Indian Joe you must follow him. If he doesn't go to the hotel, then it can't be his Number Two place."

"But I am too afraid to follow him alone, Tom!"

"It will be all right. He will not see you. If I see him, I will follow him."

■too ~ to do ～すぎて…できない

## 25. 不吉な考え

「あいつを見つけなきゃ！ 金を見つけるんだ！『2号』の場所を見つけなきゃな。家の番号かもしれないぞ」
「ちがうな、トム。この町の家には番号はついてないだろ」
「じゃあ、ホテルの部屋の番号かもしれないな」
「そうだ！ ここにはホテルは2軒しかないぞ」
「おまえはここにいろ、ハック。おれが『2号』を見つけに行く」
　トムは町へ入っていった。最初のホテルの「2号」室の部屋には、若い男が泊まっていた。
　ふたつめのホテルの「2号」室の部屋は、鍵がかかっていた。でも前の夜に、窓から明かりが見えていたそうだ。
「あの部屋がインジャン・ジョーの『2号』だ、ハック」
「きっとそうだぜ、トム。おいらたち、どうしたらいい？」
　トムは考えた。
「夜まで待って、中に入らなきゃな。おまえ、もしインジャン・ジョーを見かけたら、あとをつけるんだ。あいつがホテルに入らなかったら、あの部屋は『2号』じゃないってことだ」
「でもおいら、おっかなくて、ひとりであとをつけたりできないよ、トム！」
「大丈夫さ。気づかれやしないよ。もしおれが見かけたら、おれがつけるからさ」

# 26 Number Two
## —Huck Waits

They waited for three nights. The fourth night was very dark.
Huck stayed outside and Tom went into the hotel.
Huck waited. And waited. What had happened to Tom?
Suddenly Tom came running out of the hotel.
"Run! Run for your life!"
They ran out of town. It started to rain. They ran to an empty old building and went inside.
"Huck, I was really afraid! I opened the door and went into the room, and—Huck, I almost stepped on Indian Joe's hand!"
"No!"
"Yes! He was sleeping on the floor. Drunk, I think. I ran away."
"Tom, did you see the box?"

■for your life 命懸けで、必死で　■step on ～を踏みつける

# 26.「2号」で——ハックが待つ

　ふたりは3晩待った。4日目の夜は、とても暗かった。
　ハックが外で見張り、トムがホテルに入っていった。
　ハックは待った。さらに待った。トムに何が起こったんだろう？
　いきなり、トムがホテルから走って出てきた。
「走れ！ 命がけで走るんだ！」
　ふたりは走って町から出た。雨が降りだした。ふたりは古い空き家まで走って、中に入った。
「ハック、おれ、ほんとにこわかったよ！ ドアを開けて、部屋に入ったんだ。そしたらさ——ハック、もう少しでインジャン・ジョーの手を踏むところだったんだ！」
「なんてこった！」
「ほんとさ！ あいつ、床の上で寝てたんだ。酔っぱらってたんだと思うよ。おれ、走って逃げてきたんだ」
「トム、箱は見たか？」

## 26. Number Two—Huck Waits

"No, I did not see the box. Only drink. The room is full of drink."

"Tom, if Joe is drunk, now is the time to get the money box."

"Is it? You get it."

Huck was afraid. "No, I don't think so."

"No, let's wait until Indian Joe leaves the room. Then we can go in fast and get the box. We must watch every night."

"I agree. Let me watch all night and every night. You do the other part of the job."

"Yes, you go and watch, Huck. And when you want me, come to my window and make a sound like a cat."

■drink 名 酒類

## 26.「2号」で——ハックが待つ

「いや、箱は見なかった。酒のビンだけだった。部屋じゅう、ビンだらけさ」

「トム、ジョーが酔っぱらってるんだったらさ、いまが金貨の箱を取るチャンスじゃないか」
「そうか？ じゃ取ってこいよ」
ハックはこわくなった。「いや、やっぱりいまはダメだと思う」
「おれもだ。インジャン・ジョーが部屋を出るまで、待ってようぜ。そしたら、あっというまに入って箱を取って来れるさ。毎晩、見張らなきゃな」
「わかった。毎晩、夜中じゅうおいらが見張るよ。あとの仕事は、おまえがやってくれ」
「よし、じゃあ見張りに行ってくれ、ハック。おれに来てほしいときは、窓のところで、ネコの声で呼んでくれよな」

# 27 The Picnic
## —Indian Joe's Job

The next morning Tom heard the Thatcher family had returned. This was good news. For a while Tom forgot Indian Joe and the box of gold.

More good news. The next day there would be a picnic.

Everyone met at eleven in the morning and walked to the river. They would ride down the river on the old river-boat.

Sid was sick and did not go. Mary stayed with him.

Because it would finish late, Becky told her mother she would stay with Suzy Harper, who lived near the river.

They went down the river on the old river-boat and then stopped to eat and play by the big trees.

Then someone said, "Who wants to go into the cave?"

They took lights and entered.

Inside was very cold. The walls were rock with water running down them.

There were many rooms, big and small.

■cave 图洞窟 ■room 图空間、使える場所

# 27. ピクニック
　　——インジャン・ジョーの「仕事」

　翌朝、サッチャー家が戻ってきたとトムは耳にした。これはいい知らせだ。しばらくのあいだ、トムはインジャン・ジョーと金貨の箱のことをすっかり忘れてしまった。
　さらにいい知らせがあった。次の日に、ピクニックがあるのだという。
　みんな午前11時に集合して、川へ歩いていった。古い川船に乗って川を下るのだ。
　シッドは病気になったので行なかった。そこでメアリーが看病のために残ってくれた。
　ピクニックが終わるのは夜おそくになりそうだったので、ベッキーはお母さんに、スージー・ハーパーの家に泊まると言っておいた。スージーの家は川のそばにあるからだ。
　みんなは古い川船に乗って川を下り、大きな木のそばで船を泊めて、食べたり遊んだりした。
　そのあと、だれかが言いだした。「だれか洞窟の中に入りたくない？」
　子どもたちは明かりを持って中に入った。
　洞窟の中は、とてもひんやりしていた。ごつごつした岩壁に沿って、水が流れ落ちている。
　たくさんの横穴があって、大きいのがあれば、小さいのもあった。

## 27. The Picnic—Indian Joe's Job

No one knew all the caves. They were too big.

But Tom Sawyer knew them best.

When they went outside it was night and people were calling them. It was time to go back to the town.

Huck saw the lights of the returning river-boat. He was already watching for Indian Joe. The night was very dark. It was eleven o'clock and everyone was sleeping.

Huck also wanted to sleep.

Suddenly he heard a sound. Then he saw two men. One was carrying something. It must be the box! Should he call Tom? No. The men would walk away with the box and it would never be found again. He would follow them.

Without shoes, Huck moved as quietly as a cat.

The men went out of the town and stopped by some trees near a house.

Mrs. Douglas lived alone in the house. Huck liked Mrs. Douglas, because she was kind to him. This must be the job Indian Joe and his friend had been talking about.

"Lets go in," said Indian Joe.

"Let's forget the job."

■as ~ as …と同じくらい〜

## 27. ピクニック——インジャン・ジョーの「仕事」

　洞窟をすみずみまで知っている子はだれもいなかった。あまりに大きいからだ。
　でも、トム・ソーヤーは他のだれよりよく知っていた。
　みんなが外に出ると、もう夜になっていて、大人たちが呼んでいた。もう町に戻る時間だった。

　ハックは、戻ってくる川船の明かりを見ていた。すでにインジャン・ジョーの見張りをしているところだ。その夜はとても暗かった。午後11時で、だれもが眠りについていた。
　ハックも眠くなってきた。
　そのとたん、音がした。それからふたりの男が見えた。ひとりが何かを運んでいる。きっとあの箱だ！ トムを呼んだほうがいいかな？ いや、あいつらが箱を持っていってしまったら、もう二度と見つからないぞ。あとをつけよう。

　靴をはいていないので、ハックはネコのように音を立てずに動くことができた。
　男たちは町を出ていき、ある家のそばの木々の下で止まった。
　その家には、ダグラス夫人がひとりで住んでいた。ハックはダグラス夫人が好きだった。とてもやさしくしてくれるからだ。これが、インジャン・ジョーとその相棒が話していた「仕事」にちがいない。
　「さあ、入るぞ」とインジャン・ジョー。
　「この仕事のことは忘れようぜ」

## 27. The Picnic—Indian Joe's Job

"No. You can have the money. I do not want it. But her husband put me in jail. Then he died. I can't hurt him. But she is still living. I can hurt her."

"You must not kill her!"

"I will not kill her. I am going to cut her face. For a woman this hurts more than being killed. You will help me or I will kill you. And then I will kill her too."

Huck knew he must get help. Quietly, he went down the hill. He ran to Mr. Jones's house and hit the door.

Mr. Jones and his two strong sons opened a window and looked out.

"Who are you? What do you want?"

"Huckleberry Finn. Quick, let me come in."

They let him in. "What do you want?"

"Please never tell that I told you," were Huck's first words. "I would be killed for sure—but Mrs. Douglas has been a good friend to me. I want to tell you."

"Speak," said the old man. "We will never tell, boy."

Three minutes later the old man and his sons, carrying guns, went up the hill to Mrs. Douglas's house.

Huck ran back to the town.

■get help 助けを呼ぶ  ■come in 中に入る  ■for sure 確実に

## 27. ピクニック——インジャン・ジョーの「仕事」

「だめだ。金はおまえが取ればいいさ。おれはいらねえ。だがな、あそこの亭主がおれを牢屋にぶちこみやがったんだ。そのあと死にやがったから、亭主をやるわけにはいかねえ。でも女房は生きてるから、仕返しできるってわけさ」

「殺しちゃいけねえよ！」

「殺しゃしねえさ。顔に傷をつけてやるのさ。女にとっちゃ、顔の傷は殺されるより辛いからな。手伝わねえなら、おまえを殺すぞ。それから、あの女も殺してやるからな」

ハックは、助けを呼ばなきゃ、と思った。そして音を立てずに、丘をおりていった。ジョーンズさんの家まで走ると、ドアを叩いた。

ジョーンズさんと、ふたりのたくましい息子たちが窓を開いて外をのぞいた。

「だれだ？　なんの用だ？」

「ハックルベリー・フィンだよ。早く、中へ入れてくれよ」

ジョーンズさんはハックを家の中へ入れてやった。「いったい、なんの用だい？」

「おいらが言ったって、だれにも言わないでくれよ」というのが、ハックの最初のことばだった。「きっと殺されるからさ——でも、ダグラスさんは、おいらにとてもよくしてくれたんだ。だから言っときたいんだ」

「話してごらん」とジョーンズじいさんは言った。「だれにも言わないよ、坊や」

3分後、ジョーンズじいさんと息子たちは、銃を持って丘を登り、ダグラス夫人の家に向かった。

ハックは町へ逃げ帰った。

# 28 The Old Man Reports —Everyone is Afraid

The next day was Sunday.
　Early in the morning Huck went to the old man's house.
　"Please let me come in! It is Huck Finn."
　"That name will open this door night or day, boy!"
　The boy was surprised. He had never heard these words before.
　The old man opened the door. "Come in and have something to eat."
　"What happened last night? I heard the guns and ran away. Are the men dead?"
　"They are not dead, boy. We are sorry for that. They heard us coming, and they ran. Then we went down to the village to get help. We will look for the two men today. I wish we had seen those two men. Could you see them in the dark?"
　"Yes. One has long white hair. He can't hear and he can't talk." Then he told about the other man's face and clothes.

■night or day いつでも、昼夜を問わず

## 28. じいさんの報告
　　——みんなの心配

　次の日は日曜日だった。
　朝早くに、ハックはジョーンズじいさんの家に行った。
「入れて！ハック・フィンだよ」
「その名前を聞いたら、このドアはいつでも開くぞ、坊や！」
　少年はびっくりした。そんなことを言われたのは、生まれて初めてだった。

　じいさんはドアを開けた。「さあ入って、何か食べなさい」

「昨日の晩、どうなったの？ 銃の音が聞こえたから、おいら逃げたんだ。あいつら、死んじゃった？」
「死んでないよ、坊や。残念なことにな。わしたちが来るのを聞いて、逃げたんだ。それで、わしらは村へおりて助けを呼んだ。今日もあのふたりをさがすんだよ。あいつらの顔を見てればよかったんだがなあ。暗かったけど、あいつらが見えたかね？」
「うん。ひとりは髪が白くて長いんだ。聞こえないし、話せない」それから、ハックはもうひとりの男の顔と服装について話した。

## 28. The Old Man Reports—Everyone is Afraid

Mr. Jones asked Huck why he had followed the men up the hill.

Huck said that he thought one man was Indian Joe. But he did not tell about the box of money.

Soon people began coming to the house, and Huck went where they could not see him.

Mrs. Douglas came to thank Mr. Jones for helping her.

"You should not thank me," he said. "There is another person who did more to help you. But he does not want thanks."

Everyone went to church early that day. They wanted to talk about the two bad men who had not been found.

Leaving the church, Mrs. Thatcher walked with Mrs. Harper. She said, "Is my Becky going to sleep all day?"

"Your Becky?"

"Yes. She stayed with you last night."

"No."

Mrs. Thatcher stopped suddenly. She looked ill.

Then Aunt Polly joined them. She said, "Good morning, Mrs. Thatcher. Good morning, Mrs. Harper. Did my Tom stay with Joe last night without telling me?"

Mrs. Thatcher looked more ill than before. She moved her head, saying no.

■ill 形 気分 [具合] が悪くて

## 28. じいさんの報告──みんなの心配

　ジョーンズさんはハックに、どうしてふたりを追って丘の上まで行ったのか聞いた。
　ハックは、ひとりがインジャン・ジョーだと思ったからだと答えた。でも、金貨の箱の話はしなかった。
　やがて村の人たちが家にやってきたので、ハックは人に見られないところへ行った。
　ダグラス夫人が、ジョーンズさんに助けてもらったお礼を言いに来た。
　「わしに感謝することなんかないさ」と、じいさんは言った。「あんたをもっと助けた人間がいるんだから。でも、その本人がお礼はいらないっていうのでな」
　その日はだれもが早くに教会へ行った。みんな、まだ見つからないふたりの悪人の話をしたくてたまらないのだ。
　教会からの帰り道、サッチャー夫人はハーパー夫人と歩いていた。サッチャー夫人が言った。「うちのベッキーったら、一日じゅう寝てるつもりなのかしら？」
　「おたくのベッキーちゃん？」
　「ええ、ゆうべ、お宅に泊まらせていただいたでしょう」
　「いいえ」
　そのとたん、サッチャー夫人は立ちすくんだ。そして真っ青になった。
　そこへポリーおばさんがやってきた。おばさんは言った。「おはようございます、サッチャーさん。おはようございます、ハーパーさん。うちのトムったら、あたしにも言わないで、ジョーのお宅に泊めていただいたんですか？」
　サッチャー夫人はさっきよりもっと青くなった。そして首をふりながら、まさか、そんな、と言った。

## 28. The Old Man Reports—Everyone is Afraid

"He did not stay with us," said Mrs. Harper. She was surprised.

Aunt Polly asked Joe Harper, "Have you seen my Tom this morning?"

"No."

"When did you last see him?"

But Joe could not remember.

Suddenly everyone started talking. No one could remember Tom or Becky returning on the river-boat from the picnic. Someone said maybe they were lost in the caves.

Mrs. Thatcher and Aunt Polly began to cry.

Everyone went to look for the children.

But the next morning they were still missing.

Old Mr. Jones came home at noon and found that Huck was sick. Mrs. Douglas came to care for him.

The men looked in all parts of the cave. They shouted, but there was no answer. The strong men continued to look for three days and nights.

Huck asked about Tom Sawyer.

Mrs. Douglas said, "Quiet, child. You must not talk. You are very, very sick." She began to cry.

Everyone was afraid for Tom and Becky.

■lost 形 道に迷った　■missing 形 見つからない　■care for ～の面倒を見る

## 28. じいさんの報告――みんなの心配

「うちには泊まっていませんよ」とハーパー夫人。とても驚いているようすだ。

ポリーおばさんはジョー・ハーパーに尋ねた。「今朝、うちのトムを見なかったかい？」

「見てないよ」

「最後に見たのはいつ？」

でも、ジョーは思い出せなかった。

そのとたん、だれもが口々に話しだした。トムとベッキーがピクニックから川船で帰ってくるようすを、だれも覚えていなかった。だれかが、ふたりは洞窟で迷ったのかもしれないと言った。

サッチャー夫人とポリーおばさんが泣きだした。

人々は総出で子どもたちをさがしに行った。

だが翌朝になっても、ふたりは見つからなかった。

昼になってジョーンズじいさんが家に帰ってみると、なんとハックが病気になっていた。そこでダグラス夫人が看病しに来てくれた。

村の男の人たちが、洞窟のあらゆるところを捜索した。大声で呼んだが、返事はなかった。屈強な男たちが、3日3晩さがしつづけた。

ハックがベッドの中で、トム・ソーヤーはどうしてるか、と聞いた。

ダグラス夫人は言った。「静かにしてらっしゃい、ハック。お話はだめよ。あなたはとっても、とっても具合が悪いんですからね」そしてダグラス夫人は泣きだした。

村のだれもが、トムとベッキーのことを心配していたのだ。

# 29
## Lost, Then Found
## —But Not Saved

Tom and Becky had started walking with the other children. Then they had walked deeper and deeper into the caves. They found a small, beautiful river. Next to the river they found a new cave in the rocks. They went in and as they walked it became darker and darker. And the children became more and more afraid and started to run.

Suddenly they came to a lake and it was very quiet.

Becky said "I want to go back. Do you know the way?"

"I think so," said Tom. But the more they walked, the more lost they became.

"Tom, we are lost!" Becky said. "We will never find our way out. We will die here," she said and started to cry.

"I think I can find the way out. First we must return to the small river."

They walked and walked until they were too tired to walk any more.

■more ~, more … ～すればするほど…になる　■find one's way out　出口を見つける

# 29. 迷って見つかって
## ──でも助からなくて

　トムとベッキーは、始めのうちは他の子どもたちと一緒に歩きだした。でもそれから、洞窟の奥深く、もっと深くへと歩いていったのだ。やがて、きれいな小川が見つかった。さらに小川のそばで、岩の中に新しい横穴があるのを見つけた。ふたりはその中に入ったが、歩いていくと、だんだん暗くなってきた。そして、ますますこわくなってきたので、走りだした。

　するといきなり、湖のあるところへ出た。湖はとても静かだった。
　ベッキーが言った。「あたし、帰りたいわ。道がわかる？」
　「わかると思うよ」とトム。でも歩けば歩くほど、わからなくなっていった。

　「トム、あたしたち迷ったのよ！」とベッキーが言った。「もう出口は見つからないわ。あたしたち、ここで死ぬのよ」ベッキーはそう言って、泣きだした。
　「出口を見つけられると思うよ。まずあの小川に戻らなきゃ」

　ふたりは歩きに歩いたが、とうとう疲れはてて、もう歩けなくなった。

## 29. Lost, Then Found—But Not Saved

"I'm very hungry," Becky said. Tom had saved some cake from the picnic. He took it out of his pocket and shared it with Becky.

Then they walked some more until they found the small, beautiful river.

Tom said. "I'm sorry, I still don't know the way back."

They were tired so they quickly went to sleep. They dreamed of home and food and day-light.

They didn't know how many days had passed. Maybe a week?

"I will look again for the way out," Tom said. He moved slowly. Suddenly he saw a hand holding a light.

Tom shouted.

At once a body followed the hand. It was Indian Joe!

Tom could not move because he was afraid. Indian Joe ran away.

He did not tell Becky what he had seen or why he had shouted.

He returned to the small river. They were both tired and hungry and afraid.

Tom promised Becky he would look after her. He held her hand as they went to sleep.

But he was afraid they would not find the way out.

■save 動残しておく ■day-light 名日光 ■at once すぐに ■look after ～の面倒を見る

## 29. 迷って見つかって――でも助からなくて

「とっても、おなかがすいたわ」とベッキーが言った。トムはピクニックのケーキを少し残してあった。そこでポケットから取り出すと、ベッキーと分けあって食べた。

それからもう少し歩くと、とうとう、あのきれいな小川が見つかった。

そこでトムは言った。「ごめんよ。やっぱり帰り道はわからないよ」

ふたりは疲れていたので、あっというまに眠りに落ちた。そして家や、食べ物や、太陽の光の夢を見た。

やがて、もう何日すぎたのか、わからなくなっていった。もしかしたら、1週間だろうか？

「もういちど出口をさがしてくるよ」とトムは言った。トムはゆっくりと進んだ。するといきなり、明かりを持った手があらわれた。

トムは思わず大声をあげた。

手のあとにすぐ、体が見えてくる。インジャン・ジョーだ！

トムはこわくて動けなかった。するとインジャン・ジョーが逃げていった。

ベッキーには、何を見たか、そしてなぜ叫んだか話さないことにした。

そして小川のところに戻った。ふたりとも疲れはて、おなかがすき、こわくてたまらなかった。

トムはベッキーに、ぼくが守ってやる、と約束していた。眠るときは、ベッキーの手を握ってやった。

でもトムは、出口を見つけられないかもしれないと、ほんとうは恐れていたのだ。

# 30 Tom Tells the Story of Their Escape

Sunday and two more days had passed. A few men continued to look for the children. Most of the people thought that they would never be found.

Mrs. Thatcher was very ill. Aunt Polly's hair had changed from gray to white.

Then, one night everyone in the village began to shout.

"They are found! The children are found!"

The children were carried home. Everyone was very happy. Tom sat on his bed and told of their escape.

He had looked this way. And then he had looked that way. Suddenly he saw a light which he thought was day-light. He found a hole in the rock and could see the river. When he told Becky she didn't believe him at first. But when she saw the light and the river she was very happy.

They found some men on the river and told their story. At first the men did not believe the children.

■escape 名 脱出

# 30. トム、脱出のようすを語る

　日曜日が、そしてさらに2日がすぎた。数人の男たちが、子どもたちの捜索を続けていた。ほとんどの人が、ふたりはもう見つからないだろうと思っていた。
　サッチャー夫人は、重い病気になってしまった。ポリーおばさんの髪の毛も、灰色から真っ白に変わった。
　ところが、しばらくたったある夜のこと、村じゅうの人たちが叫びだした。
「見つかったぞ！ 子どもたちが見つかった！」
　子どもたちは家につれてこられた。みんな大喜びだった。
　トムはベッドにすわったまま、自分たちの脱出のようすについて話した。
　トムはあちらこちら、出口をさがしまわっていた。すると突然、日の光らしいものが見えた。そして岩のあいだに穴があるのを見つけ、のぞくと川が見えたのだ。ベッキーに話したけれど、最初は信じようとしなかった。でも日の光と川を見て、ベッキーは大喜びした。

　川で数人の男の人を見つけたので、自分たちのことを話した。始めのうちは、子どもたちの話を信じてくれなかった。

## 30. Tom Tells the Story of Their Escape

But then they believed the children and took them to a house where they were given food and could rest, before being taken home.

It was several days before Tom and Becky were strong again.

Tom heard that Huck was ill and went to visit him.

Mrs. Douglas would not let Tom talk about his story to Huck, because Huck was not strong enough to listen. Also, she would not let the boys talk about what had happened at her house on Cardiff Hill. Tom learned about that at home. He also heard that Indian Joe's friend had been found in the river. He had died in the river while trying to run away.

About two weeks later, Tom visited Becky at her home. Mr. Thatcher and some friends were there. They asked Tom if he wished to go into the cave again.

Tom said yes.

"Maybe other people wish to go, also." Mr. Thatcher said. "But I had the entrance closed with a metal door. It can't be opened. No one will get lost in that cave again."

"Oh, no," Tom said, "Indian Joe is in there!"

■ask someone if 〜かどうかを(人)に尋ねる　■get lost 道に迷う

## 30. トム、脱出のようすを語る

でもやがてその話がほんとうだとわかったので、家へつれていき、食べ物を与えて休ませてから、この村へつれかえってくれたのだ。

トムとベッキーがすっかり元気になるまでに、数日かかった。

元気になると、トムはハックが病気だと聞いて、見舞いに行った。
ダグラス夫人はトムに、脱出の話をハックにしないようにと言った。ハックはまだ、そんな話を聞けるほど丈夫ではなかったからだ。それに、カーディフ丘の自分の家で起こった事件についても、子どもたちに話をさせなかった。トムはそのことを家で聞いて知っていた。また、インジャン・ジョーの相棒が川で発見されたことも耳にしていた。この男は、逃亡中に川に落ちて死んだのだ。
　2週間ほどたったころ、トムはベッキーの家へ会いにいった。お父さんのサッチャーさんとその友人たちがいた。みんながトムに、また洞窟に入りたいかと尋ねた。
　トムは、もちろん、と答えた。
　「たぶん他の人たちも行きたがるだろうな」とサッチャーさんは言った。「でも、わたしが鉄の扉で入り口を閉めさせたからね。もう開けられないよ。もうだれも、あの洞窟で迷子になることはないだろう」
　「え、なんだって」とトムは言った。「あの中に、インジャン・ジョーがいるんだよ！」

# 31 What Happened to Indian Joe

Soon everyone heard the news. In a few minutes men were in boats on their way to the cave. Tom was in a boat with Mr. Thatcher.

The door was opened. Indian Joe was on the ground, dead. Tom could understand how Indian Joe had felt.

But he felt happy.

The next morning, Tom and Huck talked.

Now Huck told Tom about following Indian Joe up the hill to Mrs. Douglas's house.

"Indian Joe came from hotel Number Two," Huck said. "Now we shall never find the box of money."

"Huck," Tom said, "that money was never in the hotel. It is in the cave! Will you go there with me and help to bring it out?"

"I will as long as we do not get lost."

"Are you strong enough?" Tom asked.

"I can't walk far, Tom."

■as long as 〜である限りは、〜ということであれば

# 31. インジャン・ジョーに起こったこと

　たちまち、その知らせが村じゅうに広まった。数分後には、男たちが小舟に乗って洞窟へ向かった。トムはサッチャーさんと小舟に乗った。

　洞窟の扉が開かれた。インジャン・ジョーが地面に倒れて死んでいた。インジャン・ジョーがどんな思いをしていたか、トムにはよくわかった。
　それでも、やっぱりうれしかった。
　翌朝、トムとハックは話しあった。
　やっとハックはトムに、インジャン・ジョーのあとをつけて丘を登り、ダグラス夫人の家へ行った話をした。
　「インジャン・ジョーは、『2号』のあるホテルから来たんだ」とハックは言った。「もう金貨の箱は見つからないな」
　「ハック」とトムが言った。「金貨はホテルにあるんじゃないぜ。洞窟の中さ！　一緒に行って、運びだすのを手伝ってくれないか？」

　「迷わないんだったら、行ってもいいけどさ」
　「もうすっかり元気になったのか？」とトムは聞いた。
　「遠くまでは歩けないな、トム」

## 31. What Happened to Indian Joe

"I will take you there in a boat. It will be easy for you."

"I want to start now, Tom."

Tom agreed. "We want some bread and meat, two bags, some thread and some lights."

They went in a friend's boat. One entrance was closed but Tom knew another entrance.

The boys entered the hole. They tied the thread to a rock to guide their return. After a few steps they found the small, beautiful river. Tom was afraid. He told Huck that this was where he and Becky got lost.

The boys walked very quietly.

They continued walking and soon they came to a place where the floor ended.

Tom said: "Now I will show you something, Huck." He held his light high. "What can you see? On the big rock?"

"Tom, it is a cross!"

"That is where I saw Indian Joe, Huck. And where is Number Two? Remember what he said? 'Under the cross.'"

Huck was afraid. "Tom, I want to leave."

"What! And leave the money?"

"Yes. Leave it. Indian Joe's ghost is there."

■thread 糸

## 31. インジャン・ジョーに起こったこと

「小舟でつれてってやるよ。それならおまえも楽だろ」
「今すぐ行きたくなったぜ、トム」
トムは賛成した。「パンと肉に、袋がふたつ、糸と明かりもいるな」

ふたりは友だちの小舟に乗って出発した。ひとつの入り口は閉じられていたが、トムは別の入り口を知っているのだ。
少年たちは穴の中へ入った。糸を岩にくくりつけて、それをたどって戻るようにした。少し歩くと、きれいな小川が見つかった。トムはぞっとした。そしてハックに、ここが自分とベッキーが迷子になった場所だと言った。

少年たちは声も立てず、静かに進んだ。
歩きつづけていると、やがて突きあたりの場所へやってきた。

トムが言った。「さあ、いいものを見せてやるぜ、ハック」トムは明かりを高く持ち上げた。「何が見える？ その大きな岩の上にさ？」
「トム、十字架だ！」
「あそこがインジャン・ジョーを見た場所なんだよ、ハック。さあ、『2号』ってどこだい？ あいつがなんて言ったか覚えてるか？『十字架の下』だろ」
ハックはこわくなった。「トム、おいら、帰りたいよ」
「なんだって！ 金貨をおいてか？」
「そうだよ。おいてくんだ。あそこにはインジャン・ジョーの幽霊がいるよ」

## 31. What Happened to Indian Joe

"No, Huck. It is near the door, where he died. That is far away."

"No, Tom. His ghost would be with the money. I know about these things."

"No Huck, it would not be near a cross."

Huck agreed. "You are right Tom. We must find the box."

The boys climbed down the great rock. Tom went first, and Huck followed.

Near the great rock, the boys found where some person had been eating and sleeping. But they found no money.

They looked and found some old wood under some rocks. Behind the old wood was a small entrance. They went in.

"Huck, look there!"

It was the box of money. There were also two guns.

"We have it!" said Huck, putting his hands on the pieces of gold. "We are rich, Tom!"

"Huck, I was always sure that we would get the money. And we have it."

They put the money in two bags, and carried it back to the river.

They left the guns to get another day.

■have it 勝つ

## 31. インジャン・ジョーに起こったこと

「いるもんか、ハック。あいつが死んだのは、扉のそばだぜ。ずっと向こうだ」

「いいや、トム。あいつの幽霊なら金貨と一緒にいるんじゃないか。そういう話を知ってるぜ」

「そんなことあるもんか、ハック。あっても、十字架のそばってことはないさ」

ハックは納得した。「そのとおりだな、トム。さあ、箱をさがさなきゃ」

少年たちは大きな岩につかまりながら、おりていった。まずトムが行き、ハックがそれに続いた。

大岩のそばで、だれかが食べたり眠ったりしたあとを見つけた。でも、金貨はなかった。

見まわすと、岩の下に、古い木の板があるのに気づいた。その板の後ろに小さな入り口があった。ふたりは中に入った。

「ハック、見ろよ！」

金貨の箱だった。銃もふたつあった。

「やったぜ！」とハックが言い、金貨の上に手をおいた。「おいらたち、大金持ちだ、トム！」

「ハック、きっと金貨を手に入れられるって、いつも思ってたんだ。ついにやったぜ」

ふたりは金貨をふたつの袋に入れ、運びながら川に戻った。

銃は別の日に取りに来ることにした。

## 31. What Happened to Indian Joe

It was dark when they arrived at the village.

"Huck," said Tom, "we will take the money to Mrs. Douglas's house. I know a place near there to leave it tonight."

They borrowed a cart and took the bags of money to Cardiff Hill.

Near Mr. Jones's house they stopped to rest. Mr. Jones came out. "Who is there?" he said.

"Huck and Tom Sawyer."

"Come with me, boys. Everyone is waiting for you. Let me help. Your cart is very heavy. But it's not full of money, I am sure!"

They entered Mrs. Douglas's house.

All the important people of the village were there. The Thatcher family, the Harper family, Aunt Polly, Sid, Mary, and many more. All were dressed in their best clothes.

Tom and Huck were very dirty. Aunt Polly's face was red when she saw Tom's face and clothes.

Mrs. Douglas took the boys to a bedroom and said: "Wash and dress now. Here are new clothes for both of you. Come and join the others when you are ready."

■borrow 動 借りる

## 31. インジャン・ジョーに起こったこと

　村につくと、もうあたりは暗かった。
「ハック」とトム。「金貨をダグラスさんの家に持っていこうぜ。あのそばに、今夜これをおいとくのにいい場所があるんだ」
　ふたりは手押し車を借りて、金貨の袋をカーディフ丘へ運んだ。

　ジョーンズさんの家のそばで、ふたりは止まって休憩した。ジョーンズさんが出てきて、「そこにいるのは、だれだい？」と言った。
「ハックとトム・ソーヤーです」
「さあ、一緒においで、坊や。みんな、おまえさんたちを待ってたんだよ。さ、手伝ってやろう。ずいぶん重い荷物だね。でも金貨でいっぱいってことはないだろう、まさかな！」
　ふたりはダグラス夫人の家に入った。
　村の主だった人たちが全員そこにいた。サッチャーさんの家族、ハーパーさんの家族、ポリーおばさん、シッド、メアリー、他にもいっぱいだ。みんな晴れ着を着ている。
　トムとハックはドロドロに汚れていた。ポリーおばさんの顔は、トムの顔と服を見て真っ赤になった。
　ダグラス夫人が少年たちを寝室へつれていって、言った。「さあ、顔を洗って着がえなさい。ここにふたりの新しい服があるわ。用意できたら、みんなのところへ来てちょうだい」

# 32 Mr. Jones's Surprise is Not a Surprise

Huck said, "Tom, we can run away. We can go through the window."

"Why do you want to run away?"

"I can't join so many people, Tom."

"Don't worry. I will take care of you."

Sid came into the room.

"Sid, why are all these people here?"

"Old Mr. Jones has a surprise. It is about Huck following Indian Joe and the other man to this house. But most people already know. Someone told them." He laughed.

"I know who that was," Tom said, looking at Sid.

Some minutes later Huck and Tom were eating at a big table with the others. Then Mr. Jones stood up to speak. He told the story about Huck. It was true that people did not look surprised. But people tried to look surprised.

■take care of 〜の面倒を見る　■big table ごちそう

# 32. ジョーンズじいさんのびっくり話は、
　　びっくりじゃない

ハックが言った。「トム、逃げられるよな。窓から逃げようぜ」

「なんで逃げたいんだ？」
「こんな大勢の人の中に、おいら、いられないよ、トム」
「心配ないよ。おれがついてるから」
シッドが部屋に入ってきた。
「シッド、なんでみんな、ここに集まってるんだ？」
「ジョーンズじいさんが、びっくり話をするんだよ。ハックがインジャン・ジョーと、もうひとりの男をこの家までつけてきた話さ。でも、ほとんどの人はもう知ってるんだ。だれかが話したからね」シッドは笑った。
「だれが話したか、わかってるぞ」と、トムはシッドをにらみながら言った。
　数分後、ハックとトムは大きなテーブルで、他の人たちと一緒にごちそうを食べていた。そのときジョーンズさんが、演説しようと立ち上がった。ハックについての話をしたのだ。たしかにみんな、びっくりしていないようだった。でも驚いたふりをしようとしていた。

## 32. Mr. Jones's Surprise is Not a Surprise

Mrs. Douglas thanked Huck again and again. She said that she would give Huck a room in her house, and send him to school, and that later she would give him money to start a business.

Tom said, "Huck won't need it. He is rich."

People tried not to laugh.

Tom said, "Huck has money. I can show you." He ran outside.

Tom entered, carrying the heavy bags. He opened them and let the yellow gold fall out on the table. "Look!" he said. "Half is Huck's and half is mine."

Everyone looked. No one could speak.

Then they asked Tom to explain.

It was a long story, but everyone was interested.

There was more than twelve thousand dollars. Some of the village people owned land and were much richer than Tom and Huck. But no one had ever seen so much money at one time.

■again and again 何度も  ■own 動 所有する  ■at one time 一度に、いっぺんに

## 32. ジョーンズじいさんのびっくり話は、びっくりじゃない

　ダグラス夫人はハックに、何度も何度も感謝した。そして自分の家にハックの部屋を用意して、ハックを学校に通わせ、大きくなったら事業を始める資金を出すと言った。
　そこでトムは言った。「そんなの、ハックには必要ありません。ハックは金持ちなんです」
　人々は笑いをこらえた。
　トムは「ハックはお金を持ってるんです。見せてあげます」と言って、外に走っていった。
　やがてトムは、重い袋をかかえて家に入ってきた。そして袋を開き、金色にかがやく金貨をテーブルの上にザーッと開けた。「見てください！」とトムは言った。「半分はハックので、半分はぼくのなんです」
　だれもが目を見張った。びっくりして口もきけなかった。
　それから、みんなはトムに説明してくれとせがんだ。
　それは長い話だったが、だれもが興味津々に聞き入った。
　金貨は1万2000ドル以上あった。村の中には、土地を持っていて、トムやハックよりずっと金持ちの人もいる。でも、こんな大金を一度に目にしたことのある人は、ひとりもいなかったのだ。

# 33 Tom Makes New Plans

Tom's and Huck's money was a great thing in the poor little village. Everyone talked about it. No one could believe it.

People went looking for more money. They looked in every old, empty house.

Every word Tom and Huck spoke became important. The village newspaper had a story about Tom and Huck and everyone wanted to be friends with them.

Mrs. Douglas put Huck's money in a bank. Mr. Thatcher did the same with Tom's. Each boy had money to spend now. He had almost a dollar for every day of the year. In those days, a dollar a week was enough to buy a boy's food and clothes, and send him to school.

Mr. Thatcher liked Tom because he had saved Becky from the cave. He thought Tom would become a great man.

■a ~ a week 一週間にひとつの〜

# 33. トム、新しい計画を立てる

　トムとハックの金貨のことは、貧しい小さな村にとって一大事だった。村じゅうその話でもちきりだった。だれにとっても、信じられないような話だったのだ。
　人々はもっと金貨がないかと、さがしに行った。あらゆる古い空き家を調べまわった。
　トムとハックが話すと、どんなことばでも重要になった。村の新聞にもトムとハックの話がのり、だれもがふたりと友だちになりたがった。
　ダグラス夫人はハックの金貨を銀行に預けた。サッチャーさんが、トムの金貨も同じようにした。ふたりはそれぞれ、いま使うお金だけをもらった。その年は、毎日ほぼ1ドルもらった。そのころは、1週間に1ドルあれば、ひとりの男の子の食べ物と着るものを買い、学校へ通わせるのに十分だったのだ。

　サッチャーさんは、トムが洞窟からベッキーを救い出してくれたので、トムのことを気に入っていた。トムはきっとりっぱな人物になるだろうと思った。

## 33. Tom Makes New Plans

Huck Finn's life had changed. It was almost too great for him. Mrs. Douglas had taken him into her home. She kept him clean. Every night he had to sleep in a clean bed. He had to eat like a gentleman. He had to go to church.

He tried his new life for three weeks, and then the next day he was gone. Mrs. Douglas and all the people in the village tried to find him. They were afraid that he had died in the river.

Early on the third morning Tom Sawyer went to an old building outside the village. He found Huck. Huck had been sleeping in the building. He sat there now, smoking. His hair was wild. He was wearing his old, dirty clothes. But he looked happy.

Tom asked him to go home to Mrs. Douglas.

Huck's face became sad. He said, "Do not talk about it, Tom. I tried it. It is not for me. She is good to me, and friendly. But I can't live with her. I must get up at the same time every morning. I must wash. I must sleep in a bed. I must wear those good clothes. I can't move in those clothes. I can't sit down, I can't run, I can't play on the ground in them. I must go to church. I must wear shoes on Sunday."

"We all live like that, Huck."

## 33. トム、新しい計画を立てる

　ハック・フィンの生活はすっかり変わった。ハックにはりっぱすぎるくらいだった。ダグラス夫人はハックを自分の家に引き取った。そしてハックをいつもきれいにした。毎晩、ハックは清潔なベッドに寝なくてはならなかった。紳士のように、お行儀よく食べなければならない。教会にも行かなくてはならなかった。
　ハックは3週間、新しい生活をやってみた。でも、その次の日にいなくなってしまった。ダグラス夫人と村じゅうの人たちは、ハックをさがしまわった。川でおぼれ死んだのかもしれないと心配したのだ。
　3日目の朝早く、トム・ソーヤーは村のはずれの古い建物へ行った。トムはそこでハックを見つけた。ハックはその建物の中で寝泊りしていたのだ。いまはそこにすわって、タバコを吸っている。髪の毛はくしゃくしゃだ。古ぼけて汚い元の服を着ていた。でも幸せそうだった。

　トムは、ダグラス夫人の家へ戻るように言った。
　ハックの顔が、悲しそうにくもった。そして言った。「そのことは言わないでくれよ、トム。おいら、やってみたんだぜ。でも、おいらにゃ向いてないんだ。ダグラスさんはやさしいし、親切さ。でも一緒には暮らせないよ。おいら、毎朝おんなじ時間に起きなきゃなんないんだぜ。体を洗わなきゃなんない。ベッドで寝なきゃなんない。あの上等な服を着なきゃなんない。あんなの着たら、おいら動けないよ。床にすわっちゃいけない、走っちゃいけない、土で遊んじゃいけないだろ。教会にも行かなきゃなんない。日曜には靴をはかなきゃなんないしさ」
　「でも、みんなそうしてるんだぜ、ハック」

## 33. Tom Makes New Plans

"Tom, I am different. I can't live like that. It is too easy to get food. Mrs. Douglas won't let me smoke. And she prays all the time. I had to leave, Tom or I would die. And when school begins, I would have to go to school.

"Tom, being rich is no good. I wish I was dead all the time. I like these old clothes. I like sleeping in this place. This is what I want. Tom, I will give you my share of the money. You can give me money when I need it. But not often. I do not like what is easy to get. Please explain to Mrs. Douglas."

"Oh, Huck, you know that I can't do that. And if you try longer, you will like it."

"Like it? Yes, I will like it as if I sat on a fire! No, Tom, I won't be rich and I won't live in a house. I like the forest and the river and a place like this for sleeping. But now we are rich and all our games, like being pirates, have stopped."

"Listen, Huck. Being rich won't change that."

"Is that true, Tom?"

"It is true. But if you want to join me and the other boys and be in my club, you must live like us."

"Tom, that's not friendly."

■all the time いつも、四六時中　■share 名分け前　■as if まるで〜みたいに

## 33. トム、新しい計画を立てる

「トム、おいらはちがうんだよ。おいらは、そんなふうに暮らせない。食い物を手に入れるのだって、簡単すぎるよ。ダグラスさんはタバコを吸わせてくれないしさ。そんでもって、いっつもお祈りしてるんだぜ。出ていかなきゃならなかったんだよ、トム、でなきゃ、おいら死んじまうよ。それに学校が始まったら、学校に行かなきゃなんないだろ」

「なあトム、金持ちになるって、ちっともいいことじゃないな。いっつも死にたいくらいだよ。おいらは、このボロ服が好きなんだ。ここで寝るのが好きなんだ。これがおいらの欲しいものなんだよ。トム、おいらの分の金をおまえにやるよ。おいらが要るときに金をくれたらいいよ。でも、そんなにしょっちゅうじゃないぜ。簡単に手に入るものは、好きじゃないんだ。ダグラスさんに、わけを話しといてくれよ」

「おい、ハック、そんなことできないって、わかってるじゃないか。もう少しやってみろよ、そしたら気に入るよ」

「気に入るって？　そうだな、火の上にすわるくらいにな！　だめだよ、トム、おいらは金持ちにもならないし、家にも住まない。おいらは森と川と、こんなねぐらが好きなんだ。だけど、もう金持ちなんだから、海賊になるみたいな遊びは、みんな終わっちまうな」

「おい聞けよ、ハック。金持ちになっても、それは変わらないんだぜ」

「ほんとか、トム？」

「ほんとさ。でも、おれや他のやつらに加わって仲間になりたけりゃ、おんなじように暮らさなきゃな」

「トム、そいつはちょっと、いじわるだなあ」

## 33. Tom Makes New Plans

"I want you to join us, Huck. But all the boys who join Tom Sawyer's Club must be good, kind people."

Huck was quiet. He was thinking. After a while he said, "I will return to Mrs. Douglas for a month. I will try, if you will let me be in Tom Sawyer's Club."

"I agree, Huck. Come with me now. And I promise to ask Mrs. Douglas to change a little, Huck."

"Will you, Tom? That is good. When will you start your club?"

"Oh, soon. This evening we can have the first meeting."

"What will we do at the meeting?"

"We will promise always to help each other, and promise never to tell what we plan to do, and promise to kill any person who hurts one of us."

"I like that, Tom. I like it."

"And we must make those promises at night, in a quiet place outside the village. And sign with blood."

"This is better than being a pirate, Tom. I will stay with Mrs. Douglas. And we will have so much fun that everyone in the village will talk about us. And then Mrs. Douglas will be happy because she took me into her home."

■after a while しばらくして

## 33. トム、新しい計画を立てる

「仲間になってほしいんだよ、ハック。だけど、トム・ソーヤー団に入るすべての男子は、品行方正で親切な人じゃなきゃならないのさ」

ハックは口をつぐんだ。じっと考えている。しばらくして、ハックは言った。「おいら、1か月だけダグラスさんちに戻るよ。トム・ソーヤー団に入れてくれるなら、おいら、やってみる」

「よし、わかった、ハック。じゃあ、一緒に来いよ。ダグラスさんに少しやり方を変えてくれって頼んでやるから、約束するよ、ハック」

「ほんとか、トム？ そりゃあいいや。トム・ソーヤー団は、いつ始めるんだ？」

「ああ、すぐさ。今夜、初めての会合をしてもいいぜ」

「会合で何をやるんだ？」

「誓いを立てるのさ。いつもお互い助け合い、計画はだれにもぜったい話さないってな。それから、仲間を傷つけるやつは、どんなやつだろうと殺すって誓うんだ」

「そいつはいいな、トム。おいら、気に入ったよ」

「そんでもって、その誓いは夜にやるんだ。村のはずれの静かな場所でさ。血でサインするんだぜ」

「こりゃあ、海賊になるよりいいぞ、トム。おいら、ダグラスさんちに住むよ。そんで、おもしろいことをいっぱいやるから。村じゅうがトム・ソーヤー団の話でもちきりになるぜ。そしたらさ、ダグラスさんも、おいらを引き取ってよかったって喜んでくれるよ」

# A Few Words to End

So ends this story. Because it is the history of a boy, it must stop here. It could not go much further without becoming the history of a man.

Most of the people in this book are still living, and are happy. Some day the story may continue. But for now, it will stop.

■go further さらに進める

# 終わりのことば

　これで、この話は終わりです。少年の物語なので、ここで終わりにしなければなりません。これ以上先へ進むと、大人の物語になってしまいますから。

　この本に出てくる人々のほとんどは、いまも元気で幸せに暮らしています。いつの日か、話の続きを書くことがあるかもしれません。でも今のところは、これで終わることにしましょう。

## 覚えておきたい英語表現

> You will help me or I will kill you. (p.200, 6行目)
> 手伝わねえならお前を殺すぞ。

【解説】orはA or Bなどで「AかBか」という意味をよくご存じのことと思いますが、もう一つぜひ覚えていただきたい意味が「さもないと…」です。命令文、もしくは勧告・提案とともによく使われます。

【例文】　Take a taxi, or you'll miss the train.
　　　　　タクシーに乗りなさい、さもないと列車に乗り遅れますよ。

　　　　　Don't move, or I'll shoot you!　動くな、さもないと撃つぞ！

　　　　　You should study harder, or you will fail in the examination.
　　　　　もっと一生懸命勉強しなさい、さもないと試験に失敗しますよ。

> But the more they walked, the more lost they become. (p.208, 9行目)
> しかし歩けば歩くほど、さらに迷ってしまった。

【解説】the + 比較級を見たらこのパターンを思い出して下さい。慣れておくと便利な表現です。

【例文】　*The deeper* you dive, *the higher* the water pressure becomes.
　　　　　深く潜れば潜るほど、水圧が高くなる。

　　　　　*The more* I stare you, *the more* I love you.
　　　　　君を見つめれば見つめるほど、ますます君が恋しくなる。

> They were too tired to walk any more. (p.208, 下から2行目)
> 彼らは疲れ果ててしまい、もう歩けなかった。

【解説】too 〜は「〜過ぎる」という意味です。文全体を直訳すると「彼らはそれ以上歩くには疲れすぎていた」となります。

【例文】 The coffee was too hot to drink. そのコーヒーは熱すぎて飲めなかった。

to V がなくても「〜できない」を含意することがあります。

【例文】 The computer is too expensive for me.
そのパソコンは私には高すぎる。（だから買えない）

This dress is too large for you.
このドレスはあなたには大きすぎる。（だから着用できない）

ちなみに p.232、1行目のハックルベリー・フィンの台詞に "It is too easy to get food." という台詞もあります。こちらもしっかりチェックしておいて下さい。

> I do not like what is easy to get. （p.232, 8行目）
> おいらは簡単に手に入るものは好きじゃないんだ。

【解説】what は関係代名詞で「もの、こと」と訳せばよいですから、"what is easy" で「簡単なもの・こと」という意味です。be easy to V で「V するのが簡単」です。

【例文】 I can't understand what you said.
私はあなたが言ったことが理解できない。

　それにしてもなんともハックルベリー・フィンらしさが込められた台詞ではありませんか。トムたちは様々ないたずらや冒険を経験して少しずつ大人になっていきます。読者はハックを説得するトムの台詞にほんの少し大人になったトムの成長を感じることでしょう。しかしハックはまだまだ子どもらしさ、ひいては自分らしさを捨てきれずにいます。
　「そうありたいけど、いつまでもそのままではいられない」……そんな誰もが経験した大人への階段がトムたちの目の前に迫ってきているようです。マーク・トウェインの「終わりのことば」と合わせて噛みしめたい場面です。
　誰もが気になるハックの今後ですが、"The Adventures of Tom Sawyer" の9年後、1885年に "Adventures of Huckleberry Finn" としてその冒険が語られることになります。

[IBC対訳ライブラリー]
英語で読むトム・ソーヤーの冒険

2014年5月6日　第1刷発行

原 著 者　マーク・トウェイン
英語解説　出水田隆文

発行者　浦　晋亮

発行所　IBCパブリッシング株式会社
　　　　〒162-0804 東京都新宿区中里町29番3号　菱秀神楽坂ビル9F
　　　　Tel. 03-3513-4511　Fax. 03-3513-4512
　　　　www.ibcpub.co.jp

印刷所　株式会社シナノパブリッシングプレス

© IBC Publishing, Inc. 2014

Printed in Japan

落丁本・乱丁本は、小社宛にお送りください。送料小社負担にてお取り替えいたします。
本書の無断複写（コピー）は著作権法上での例外を除き禁じられています。

ISBN978-4-7946-0276-3